Taxcafe.co.uk Tax Guides

Using a Company to Save Tax

By Nick Braun PhD

Important Legal Notices:

Taxcafe®
TAX GUIDE - 'Using a Company to Save Tax'

Published by:
Taxcafe UK Limited
67 Milton Road
Kirkcaldy
KY1 1TL
Tel: (0044) 01592 560081

15th Edition, July 2014

ISBN: 978-1-907302-89-3

Disclaimer
Before reading or relying on the content of this tax guide please read the disclaimer.

Disclaimer

About the Author & Taxcafe

Dr Nick Braun founded Taxcafe in 1999, along with his partner Aileen Smith. As the driving force behind the company, they aim to provide affordable plain-English tax information for private individuals, business owners and professional advisors.

Over the past 14 years Taxcafe has become one of the best-known tax publishers in the UK and has won several prestigious business awards.

Nick has been a specialist tax writer since 1989, first in South Africa, where he edited the monthly *Tax Breaks* publication, and since 1999 in the UK, where he has authored several tax books including *Property Capital Gains Tax*, *Small Business Tax Saving Tactics* and *Pension Magic*.

Nick also has a PhD in economics from the University of Glasgow, where he was awarded the prestigious William Glen scholarship and later became a Research Fellow.

Contents

Contents (cont...)

Contents (cont...)

Introduction

Using a company could easily save you over £10,000 in tax *every year*...possibly over £40,000.

There are several reasons why companies are such powerful tax shelters.

First of all, while sole traders and partnerships pay income tax and national insurance on their profits, companies only pay corporation tax – and corporation tax rates are often much lower than personal tax rates.

For example, small companies with profits under £300,000 pay corporation tax at just 20%. By contrast, sole traders and partners who earn over £41,865 pay 42% income tax and national insurance. Those with income over £150,000 pay 47% tax.

A company paying tax at just 20% will therefore have a lot more money left over to reinvest and grow than a sole trader or partnership paying tax at 42% or 47%.

Another reason why using a company is so attractive is because, unlike other self-employed people, company owners are in the fortunate position of wearing two caps. On the one hand, you can reward your hard work as a *director*; on the other, you can reward your entrepreneurship as a *shareholder*.

As a company director and shareholder you can split your income into salary and dividends, generating large income tax and national insurance savings. For example, while national insurance is payable on salaries, it is not payable on shareholder dividends.

Not only can you decide whether any distribution of the company's money is classified as salary or dividend, as a company owner you have complete control over *how much* income you withdraw in total.

This gives you significant control over your personal tax bill, allowing you to avoid the higher tax rates that kick in when your income exceeds £41,865, £50,000, £100,000 or £150,000. Sole traders cannot control their income tax bills in this way.

Some of the subjects covered in this guide include:

- All relevant tax changes made in the March 2014 Budget.
- A plain-English guide to how companies are taxed.
- Detailed examples showing the exact amount of tax **you** could save by using a company.
- How to avoid paying any national insurance as a company owner.
- The tax benefits of dividends, including how to pay them correctly and avoid trouble from the taxman.
- How company owners can increase their tax savings by tens of thousands of pounds by keeping money inside their companies.
- How to save thousands more in tax by bringing your spouse or partner into the company.
- How company owners can protect their child benefit payments.
- How company owners can pay less capital gains tax when they sell buy-to-let properties and other assets.
- The *non-tax* benefits and drawbacks of using a company.
- The benefits and drawbacks of owning multiple companies.
- How to incorporate an existing business, including how to avoid capital gains tax and stamp duty land tax.
- A guide to future tax changes.

The guide also contains many useful tables that show the exact tax savings that can be enjoyed by company owners at every profit level. These tables take account of all taxes: income tax, corporation tax, national insurance etc.

The guide also examines a variety of other important tax issues facing company owners, including:

- Pension contributions
- Home office expenses
- Travel expenses
- Motoring expenses
- Tax treatment of losses
- Selling the business
- Business property
- Borrowing money

There has been much speculation in recent years that the Government will end the significant benefits of using a company.

However, politicians and governments have come and gone and, while there have been changes, using a company to save tax is as attractive as ever!

Using This Guide & Limitations

This tax guide deals primarily with the 2014/15 tax year, which starts on 6 April 2014 and finishes on 5 April 2015. There are references to other tax years, however it is important to emphasise that the tax rates and tax laws that will apply in future tax years are not known with any degree of certainty.

Tax rates and tax laws (including HMRC's interpretation of those laws) are continually changing. The reader must bear this in mind when reading this guide.

My purpose in writing this guide is to explain in plain English the tax benefits and drawbacks of using a company. Please note that this is NOT supposed to be a do-it-yourself (DIY) tax planning guide. If you are thinking of setting up a company I strongly recommend that you obtain professional advice after reading this guide.

Furthermore, although the guide covers a fair amount of ground, it does not cover every possible scenario and angle. Businesses and their owners come in many different shapes and sizes, so it is possible that the information contained in this guide will not be relevant to your circumstances.

There are also non-tax factors that have to be considered when deciding whether or not to use a company and these may be as important or more important that the tax issues.

For all of these reasons it is vital that you obtain professional advice before taking any action based on information contained in this guide. The author and Taxcafe UK Ltd cannot accept any responsibility for any loss which may arise as a consequence of any action taken, or any decision to refrain from taking action, as a result of reading this guide.

Part 1

Non-Tax Benefits & Drawbacks

Chapter 1

Company Benefits

Arguably the most important reason for setting up a company is to save tax. However, there are many other benefits which have nothing to do with cutting your tax bill. Although they are not the focus of this guide, it's worth mentioning them in brief:

Limited Liability Protection

In layman's language, this means that a company's owners and directors are not responsible for the company's debts and cannot be sued by outsiders.

If the company goes bust your *personal* assets are safe. (You do, however, stand to lose the money you've invested in the company and any assets you've transferred to the company.)

This legal protection comes about because the company and its owners are separate legal entities in the eyes of the law. In legal terms this is often known as the 'veil of incorporation', with the company providing a barrier separating its assets from the shareholder's personal assets.

In practice, much of the limited liability benefit will be taken away by cautious lenders and suppliers. For example, banks will usually not lend money to small companies unless the directors or shareholders provide personal guarantees.

Furthermore, the directors may be held personally liable for losses resulting from their own illegal acts or if they act negligently or beyond their powers.

Directors can be held personally liable for the company's debts if there has been wrongful trading, i.e. if they know or should have known that there was no reasonable prospect of the debts being repaid because the company is in financial trouble.

The courts may intervene and 'pierce the corporate veil', holding those who control the company personally responsible, if the company is used as a device to commit fraud or to escape legal obligations.

In the case of *Gilford Motor Co Ltd v Horne*, the former employee of a car company (Mr Horne) set up a new company in his wife's name in an attempt to circumvent a non-compete clause in his previous employer's employment contract. The court granted an injunction against Mr Horne and the new company because the new company was formed merely to mask his activities.

In another case, *VTB v Nutritek*, the court confirmed that the corporate veil can only be pierced in these circumstances when there is some 'impropriety'. The company's involvement in any impropriety will not by itself justify piercing the veil – the impropriety 'must be linked to use of the company structure to avoid or conceal liability'.

In summary, limited liability protection could prove useful when the business faces unexpected losses or legal liabilities but will not protect you in all circumstances.

Finally, it should be noted that limited liability status can also be obtained by using a limited liability partnership (LLP).

Enhanced Status

Trading as a company is often seen as more prestigious than trading in your own name. Many people will have more faith in a business called Joe Bloggs Limited rather than just plain Joe Bloggs. Of course, it makes virtually no difference in practice whether a business is incorporated or not.

Borrowing Money

Corporate status seems to be a positive factor in the eyes of some lenders and may make it easier to obtain credit from suppliers. However, in reality, a newly formed company will probably struggle to obtain credit or borrow money without personal guarantees from the directors/shareholders.

Sole traders rely on their own personal credit ratings if they wish to borrow money for the business. If the business owner's personal credit rating deteriorates, this will affect the ability of the business to borrow.

Companies, on the other hand, have their own credit scores. However, these take time to build. For example, a lender may wish to see several years' worth of accounts before handing over any money.

Companies may, however, find it easier than sole traders and other unincorporated businesses to raise funds by issuing shares in the company to new investors.

An unincorporated business also cannot raise a 'floating charge' over its assets, whereas a company can. (With a floating charge the lender's claim is lodged over all of the assets, both present and future, rather than one specific asset. This leaves the borrower free to sell, buy and vary the assets within the group.)

Equity finance is also available to companies and there are schemes such as the Enterprise Investment Scheme (EIS) and Seed Enterprise Investment Scheme (SEIS) that can provide tax relief to the providers of the finance.

Flexibility of Ownership

Using a company makes it easy to involve new people in the ownership of the business and to separate ownership and management.

For example, if you want to involve your adult children or key employees, you can issue them with shares. Using a company allows you to provide small parcels of ownership quite easily.

If you want to keep your stake in the business but do not want to be involved in its day to day management, you can keep your shares but resign as a director.

Similarly, passing the business on to family members can be easier if you use a company as you can leave shares to a number of different beneficiaries.

There are specific tax reliefs available for transferring shares in trading companies (but not investment companies).

Therefore if you want to involve younger family members in the business you can frequently transfer shares to them free of UK tax by taking advantage of the various tax reliefs.

Continuity

It's something almost nobody setting up a business thinks about but is probably the most important decision facing business owners close to retirement: succession.

A company structure allows for a smooth exit from the company. Small parcels of shares can be passed on to family members over a number of years.

The death of a company member does not affect the existence of the company.

Chapter 2

Company Drawbacks

Using a company is not always in your best interests and it's worth pointing out some of the non-tax drawbacks (tax drawbacks are covered in Part 7 and elsewhere):

Costs

It costs virtually nothing to set up a company. All you have to do is go to one of the many company formation experts and they'll do most of the work for just a few hundred pounds.

Where you will incur higher costs is in ongoing accountancy fees. Most accountants charge companies more than sole traders and partnerships because of the extra requirement to prepare and file accounts with Companies House. Company accounts need to be filed in a prescribed format and often need to be prepared in accordance with various financial reporting standards.

In many (but not all) cases, the tax savings will cover these extra fees.

Company Law

As a company director you will be subject to UK company law. This may restrict your ability to use the company's funds for private purposes.

Fortunately, most small companies no longer have to undergo expensive and time-consuming audits of their annual accounts.

Small private companies are now exempt from mandatory audits if they meet at least two of the following criteria:

- No more than 50 employees
- No more than £3.26 million of gross assets
- No more than £6.5 million turnover

Reporting Requirements

When you operate as a company your annual accounts have to be filed with Companies House. These will reveal financial information about your company. However, small companies only need to file an abbreviated balance sheet. These documents will tell the outside world relatively little about your dealings.

Accounts must be filed within 9 months of the end of the financial year and there are penalties for late filing.

Company directors are also obliged to keep minutes of directors' meetings, and to comply with statutory filing obligations. Every year an annual return has to be filed with Companies House but, unless there have been significant changes to the company's ownership or structure, this is essentially a 10-minute exercise. There is a small annual filing fee (currently £40, unless you file online in which case it is £13).

PAYE

PAYE applies to any business that has employees and therefore affects both limited companies and unincorporated businesses. The difference between companies and sole traders is that the sole trader himself will not be an employee and is therefore not subject to PAYE.

In a limited company setting, the chances are that the owners of the business will also be directors and therefore PAYE may need to be deducted from any salaries paid to them, with the added requirement to make regular submissions of information to HMRC.

An accountant or payroll provider can do all the work for you but you will probably end up paying at least a couple of hundred pounds per year for even the smallest husband and wife company.

Part 2

Why Companies Are Excellent Tax Shelters

Chapter 3

Why You and the Company Aren't Really Separate

This is the shortest chapter in this guide but the message is an important one.

Although you and your company are separate legal entities, it always amazes us how many authors write about companies and their owner/managers as if they are completely separate. What nonsense!

As a company owner you care very much about how the company's money is spent. It is in reality – no matter what the textbooks say – YOUR money.

As a shareholder you have the ultimate say as to whether it goes to pay for your holiday or is simply given away to charity. Nobody else can tell you what to do with the company's money except in very exceptional circumstances.

In practice, therefore, you and your company are not really separate.

Why are we even mentioning this? Because throughout this guide, when we compare the tax treatment of companies and unincorporated businesses, we are interested in the **whole** picture.

We do not just look at the company's tax position in isolation from you, the owner/director.

We also do not look at your personal tax in isolation from the company's tax bill. We look at both as a single unit. This is the only way to compare doing business through a company with doing business as a sole trader or partnership.

Doing something that decreases your personal tax bill is not much use if it has an adverse effect on the company's tax position. It's your company, so in reality the company's tax bill is your tax bill.

Although there are special tax and other laws that affect you and the company differently, ultimately your aim is to use these to best advantage to improve your personal financial position.

There are many detailed examples of tax savings in this guide. Note that all of these examples take into account the tax position of both the company and its owners. So we may be including many taxes in the mix: corporation tax, income tax, capital gains tax and national insurance.

Chapter 4

Company Tax Basics

When it comes to tax, the most important difference between companies and other businesses can be summarised as follows:

Self-employed businesses (sole traders and partnerships) pay <u>income tax</u> and <u>national insurance</u> on their profits and <u>capital gains tax</u> on their capital gains.

Companies pay <u>corporation tax</u> on both their income and capital gains.

In this chapter I will explain how corporation tax is calculated. Despite all the mumbo-jumbo in tax textbooks, it's actually quite simple in most cases. In Chapter 7 we'll look at how sole traders and partnerships are taxed and in later chapters we'll compare the tax paid by company owners and the self employed.

Corporation Tax Rates

There are currently two 'official' corporation tax rates. For the financial year commencing 1 April 2014 the rates are as follows:

- Small profits rate   20%
- Main rate   21%

Companies with taxable profits of £300,000 or less pay 20% corporation tax and companies with taxable profits exceeding £1.5 million pay 21% tax.

If profits are between £300,000 and £1.5 million a 'marginal relief' calculation is made. The practical effect of this is that there are effectively three corporation tax rates:

Profits up to £300,000	20%
Profits from £300,000 to £1.5 million	21.25%
Profits over £1.5 million	21%

For example, a company with profits of £400,000 for the year ending 31 March 2015 will pay 20% on the first £300,000 of profits and 21.25% on the remaining £100,000.

A company with profits of £1.5 million will pay 20% tax on the first £300,000 and 21.25% on the remaining £1.2 million. The total corporation tax bill will be £315,000 and the company's overall effective tax rate will be 21%:

$$£315,000/£1,500,000 = 21\%$$

So once profits exceed £1.5 million, you can ignore the 20% and 21.25% tax rates. All profits are taxed at a single rate of 21%.

It doesn't get much easier than this!

Future Corporation Tax Changes

No changes to the 20% small profits rate have been announced. However, the main rate will fall to 20% in April 2015.

In other words, starting in April 2015 all companies will pay 20% corporation tax, no matter how much profit they make.

The past, current and future corporation tax rates can be summarised as follows:

Profits	Year Commencing 1 April		
	2013	2014	2015
Up to £300,000	20%	20%	20%
£300,000 to £1.5 million	23.75%	21.25%	20%
Over £1.5 million	23%	21%	20%

Just a few years ago the main rate was 30% and the marginal rate on profits between £300,000 and £1.5 million was a whopping 32.5%!

The reduction in corporation tax rates should provide a welcome boost to bigger companies. Paying tax at 20% instead of 32.5% means they will have more after-tax profit to reinvest or pay out as dividends.

The reduction in corporation tax may also encourage more business owners to set up companies. The top tax rate for self-employed business owners is currently 47% – *more than double* the 20% all companies will pay from 2015 onwards.

Marginal Rate Planning

The reduction in corporation tax rates in recent years has also reduced the importance of 'marginal rate' tax planning – keeping profits below £300,000 to avoid a much higher corporation tax rate.

For example, a few years ago if you expected your company to make profits of £330,000 you may have chosen to get the company to make a £30,000 contribution to your pension or to incur other tax-deductible expenditure. This would have attracted additional corporation tax relief of up to £3,750 (at 32.5% instead of 20%).

At present, with a top marginal corporation tax rate of 21.25%, this type of tax planning yields miniscule tax savings: £375 (£30,000 x 1.25%).

From April 2015, when the flat 20% corporation tax rate is introduced, this type of tax planning will yield no additional tax savings and companies will have no need to go to extra lengths to keep their profits below £300,000.

Accounting Periods vs Financial Years

A company's own tax year (also known as its 'accounting period') may end on any date, for example 31 December, 31 March etc.

Corporation tax, on the other hand, is calculated according to financial years. Financial years run from 1 April to 31 March.

The 2014 financial year is the year starting on 1 April 2014 and ending on 31 March 2015.

Why is this important? For starters, it's often useful to be aware of the official terminology, for example when talking to your accountant or when reading HMRC's official documentation.

It may also be important when calculating how much tax your company will pay, especially when corporation tax rates change from one financial year to the next.

For example, on 1 April 2014 the main rate of corporation tax fell from 23% to 21%. A company with over £1.5 million of taxable profits, whose accounting period runs from January 2014 to December 2014, will therefore pay corporation tax as follows:

- 3 months to 31 March 2014   23%
- 9 months to 31 December 2014   21%

The practical effect is that the company will pay 23% corporation tax on approximately one quarter of its profits and 21% tax on three quarters of its profits. (It doesn't matter at what point during the financial year the profits are actually made.) This means the company's effective corporation tax rate is 21.5%.

Companies with profits of £300,000 or less pay corporation tax at the small profits rate. The rate is currently 20% and no changes have been announced for future years. So for these companies it is not necessary to do two corporation tax calculations. Corporation tax will be payable at a flat rate of 20% on all of the company's profits, even if the accounting period straddles two financial years.

Chapter 5

Owning More than One Company: Benefits & Drawbacks

Company owners often think about setting up a second company, to keep a new venture separate from an existing business.

Often there are sound commercial reasons for using more than one company, including to:

- Limit liability
- Involve different shareholders
- Enable a stand-alone sale of the new business

Associated Companies – Corporation Tax

Having more than one company can have adverse corporation tax effects, although these will largely disappear from April 2015.

At present, the corporation tax profit bands must be divided up if there are any 'associated companies'. The basic rule is that a company is associated with another company if they are both under the control of the same person.

For example, if you own all of the shares in two companies these companies will be associated. Each company will start paying corporation tax at 21.25% when its profits exceed £150,000 (i.e. £300,000/2). If there are three associated companies, this higher rate will kick in at £100,000 (£300,000/3)... and so on.

When Companies Are Not Associated

You don't have to count companies that are not carrying on a business. This means dormant companies are disregarded, as are companies that only receive interest from a bank account. Similarly, a company that exists only to hold property (e.g. a second home overseas) and does not rent out the property does not usually need to be counted as an associated company.

Shares Owned by Family Members

Shares owned by your 'associates' can be treated as your own when deciding if two companies are associated. Associates include your close relatives (your spouse, parents, children, grandchildren and brothers and sisters) and business partners.

However, shares owned by your associates generally only need to be counted if there is a substantial commercial relationship between the companies.

Corporation Tax Reform

The associated company rules will become much less important in April 2015 when the main rate of corporation tax is reduced to 20% and unified with the small profits rate.

Business owners will no longer have an incentive to spread their activities across several companies to avoid paying corporation tax at the main rate. A few years ago, when the main rate was 30% and the small profits rate was 19%, there was an incentive to own lots of small companies rather than one large one.

By the same token, owning multiple associated companies will not result in a corporation tax rate penalty: they will all pay 20% tax on all of their profits.

The associated company rules will still be relevant for other purposes, for example in deciding whether a company has to pay corporation tax in quarterly instalments. Instalments are generally payable by companies whose profits exceed £1.5 million but this amount is divided up if there are any associated companies.

Whereas small companies only have to pay their corporation tax nine months after the financial year has ended, companies subject to instalments have to start paying tax half way through the year.

The associated company rules will be replaced with a simpler "51% group test" in April 2015. If a company owns at least 51% of, say, three subsidiaries, the four companies will be "associated" and the £1.5 million profit limit will be divided by four to determine whether corporation tax has to be paid in instalments.

£2,000 Employment Allowance

Most businesses qualify for the new employment allowance, which provides a saving of up to £2,000 per year in employer's national insurance.

However, a company cannot claim the employment allowance if a 'connected company' already claims it. Companies are connected if one company has control of the other company or both companies are controlled by the same person.

A person is generally considered to have control of a company if they hold more than 50% of the company's share capital or voting power or if they are entitled to more than 50% of the company's distributable income or assets if the company is wound up.

For example, if you own all the shares in two companies you will only be entitled to one employment allowance, even if the two companies are completely separate businesses with, for example, separate premises and staff.

If the company that claims the employment allowance has employer's class 1 national insurance of less than £2,000, the balance cannot be claimed by the other company.

Where there is 'substantial commercial interdependence' between two or more companies the holdings of close relatives and other 'associates' are added together to determine whether they are controlled by the same person or group of persons.

For example, if you own all the shares in company X and your spouse owns all the shares in company Y, your spouse's holding in company Y is attributed to you and you are treated as controlling company X and Y, as is your spouse. However, the two companies will only be treated as connected companies if there is substantial commercial interdependence between them.

If the two companies are completely unrelated then two employment allowances can be claimed. If there is substantial commercial interdependence between the companies then only one allowance can be claimed.

The definition of associates is broad but would typically include spouses, parents and grandparents, children and grandchildren, brothers and sisters, business partners and certain trusts.

To determine whether there is substantial commercial interdependence between two companies one or more of the following must be present:

- **Financial interdependence** – Two companies are financially interdependent if one gives financial support to the other or each has a financial interest in the same business.

- **Economic interdependence** – Two companies are economically interdependent if they have the same economic objective or the activities of one benefits the other or they have common customers.

- **Organisational interdependence** – Two companies are organisationally interdependent if they have common management, employees, premises or equipment.

Finally, please note that throughout this guide, the focus is mainly the tax position of a single trading company with no active associated companies.

Chapter 6

Trading Companies versus Investment Companies

In tax jargon a 'trading' company is one involved in, for want of a better word, 'regular' business activities, e.g. a company that sells goods online, a catering company or a firm of garden landscapers.

Common types of non-trading company include those that hold substantial investments in property or financial securities or earn substantial royalty income.

Corporation Tax

If your company is involved 'wholly or mainly' in non-trading activities it could be classed as a close investment holding company (CIC).

CICs pay corporation tax at the main rate, currently 21%, on ALL of their profits, including their existing trading profits. They cannot benefit from the 20% small profits rate.

Of course, with a mere 1% difference between the main rate and small profits rate, this is no longer much of a penalty and will be irrelevant from April 2015 when the two corporation tax rates are merged.

Companies that invest in rental property are specifically excluded from the CIC provisions. This means they can enjoy the 20% corporation tax rate (unless there is private use of the properties by the owner and his family or they are let to connected persons).

Capital Gains Tax

If a company has too many non-trading activities (including most property investment and property letting) it may lose its trading status for capital gains tax purposes.

This will result in the loss of two important CGT reliefs:

- Entrepreneurs Relief
- Holdover Relief

Entrepreneurs Relief allows you to pay capital gains tax at just 10% when you sell your company, as opposed to 28% (see Chapter 25).

Holdover Relief allows you to give shares in the business to children, common-law spouses and other individuals free from CGT. (You don't need Holdover Relief to transfer shares to your spouse because such transfers are always exempt.)

Although owning rental properties will not affect the company's corporation tax rate, it can affect the company's CGT rate.

The company will, however, only lose its trading status for CGT purposes if it has 'substantial' investment activities. Unfortunately to the taxman 'substantial' means as little as 20% of various measures such as:

- Assets
- Turnover
- Expenses
- Profits
- Directors' and employees' time

HMRC may attempt to apply the 20% rule to any of the above measures.

Inheritance Tax

Shares in trading companies generally qualify for business property relief which means they can be passed on free from inheritance tax. However, if the company holds investments (including rental property) this could result in the loss of business property relief.

The qualification criteria are, however, more generous than for CGT purposes and a company generally only loses its trading status for inheritance tax purposes if it is 'wholly or mainly' involved in investment related activities.

To be on the safe side you may want to ensure that the company's qualifying activities exceed 50% of each of the measures listed above (e.g. turnover, time, profits etc).

For more information see our guide *How to Save Inheritance Tax*.

Incorporating an Existing Business

One of the key tax issues when incorporating an *existing* business is whether capital gains tax can be avoided when the business is transferred into the company. In general only trading activities qualify for capital gains tax deferral on incorporation. A non-trading activity may result in a significant tax bill.

Chapter 7

How the Self-Employed Are Taxed

Self-employed business owners (sole traders and partnerships) pay income tax and national insurance on their taxable profits:

Income Tax

For the current 2014/15 tax year most self-employed individuals pay income tax as follows:

- 0%   on the first   £10,000   Personal allowance
- 20%   on the next   £31,865   Basic-rate band
- 40%   above   £41,865   Higher-rate threshold

Generally speaking, if you earn more than £41,865 you are a higher-rate taxpayer; if you earn less you are a basic-rate taxpayer.

Income over £100,000

When your income exceeds £100,000 your personal allowance is gradually reduced. It is reduced by £1 for every £2 you earn above £100,000. So once your income reaches £120,000 you will have no personal allowance left at all.

This is bad news for those earning over £100,000. The personal allowance currently saves you £4,000 in tax if you're a higher-rate taxpayer.

Example

Bill has self-employment income of £110,000. His earnings exceed the £100,000 limit by £10,000. This means his personal allowance will be reduced by half this amount (£5,000), leaving him with a personal allowance of £5,000.

It's important to note that the £5,000 of income that was tax free will now be taxed at 40%, not 20%. The basic-rate tax band is limited to just £31,865 of income.

In summary, Bill pays income tax at the following rates:

First £5,000	*0%*
Next £31,865	*20%*
Next £73,135	*40%*

Paying Tax at 60%

Anyone earning between £100,000 and £120,000 faces a marginal income tax rate of 60%. This can be illustrated with the following example.

Example

Caroline, a sole trader, has earned taxable income of £100,000 so far during the current tax year.

If she receives an extra £100 of income she will pay an extra £40 of income tax. She will also lose £50 of her income tax personal allowance, so £50 of previously tax-free income will now be taxed at 40%, adding £20 to her tax bill.

All in all, she pays £60 in tax on her extra £100 of income, so her marginal income tax rate is 60%.

Income above £150,000

Once your taxable income exceeds £150,000, you will pay 45% income tax on any extra self-employment income. This is known as the additional rate of tax. It used to be 50%.

Self-employed taxpayers pay the same income tax as salary earners (including company owners who pay themselves salaries) but the national insurance position is completely different.

National Insurance 2014/15

Self-employed business owners usually pay class 4 national insurance as follows:

- 0%   on the first   £7,956
- 9%   on the next   £33,909
- 2%   above   £41,865

Most self-employed individuals with annual earnings over the £5,885 'small earnings exception' must also pay class 2 national insurance of £2.75 per week – £143 for the year.

Certain types of income are not subject to national insurance, including interest from bank accounts (including business bank accounts) and rental income.

Combined Tax Rates 2014/15

Putting all of the above income tax and national insurance rates together, we can see that most self-employed business owners face the following combined marginal tax rates in 2014/15:

First £5,885	£0
£5,885 to £7,956	£143
£7,956 to £10,000	9%
£10,000 to £41,865	29%
£41,865 to £100,000	42%
£100,000 to £120,000	62%
£120,000 to £150,000	42%
Over £150,000	47%

Chapter 8

Companies as Tax Shelters

So which tax rates are better – the corporation tax rates outlined in Chapter 4 or the self-employment tax rates outlined in the previous chapter?

Let's say Joe Bloggs Limited has taxable profits of just £10,000. The company will pay £2,000 in corporation tax (£10,000 x 20%). But what if Joe Bloggs is a sole trader? Putting £10,000 into the table of combined tax rates on the previous page produces a tax bill of £327. The company's tax bill is £1,673 higher than the sole trader's.

Why? Small companies pay 20% tax on ALL their profits, even if those profits amount to just a few hundred pounds. Sole traders, on the other hand, can receive up to £10,000 free from income tax and up to £7,956 free from national insurance.

Thanks to these tax-free allowances, when profits are low self-employed individuals pay less tax than companies.

However, when profits exceed £10,000, self-employed individuals start paying tax at 29%, compared with the 20% paid by companies.

The threshold is currently £28,600: when profits are less than £28,600 a sole trader will pay less tax than a company; when profits exceed £28,600 a company will pay less tax than a sole trader.

When profits reach £41,865 the sole trader becomes a higher-rate taxpayer and starts paying tax at 42%, whereas the company continues paying tax at 20%. As a result, the savings from using a company start to accelerate.

For example, when profits reach £50,000 the company's tax bill will be £2,985 lower than the sole trader's and when profits reach £80,000 the company's tax bill will be £9,585 lower.

TABLE 1
Corporation Tax vs Sole Trader Tax 2014/15

Profits £	Corporation Tax £	Sole Trader £	Saving £
10,000	2,000	327	-1,673
20,000	4,000	3,227	-773
30,000	6,000	6,127	127
40,000	8,000	9,027	1,027
50,000	10,000	12,985	2,985
60,000	12,000	17,185	5,185
70,000	14,000	21,385	7,385
80,000	16,000	25,585	9,585
90,000	18,000	29,785	11,785
100,000	20,000	33,985	13,985
110,000	22,000	40,185	18,185
120,000	24,000	46,385	22,385
130,000	26,000	50,585	24,585
140,000	28,000	54,785	26,785
150,000	30,000	58,985	28,985
160,000	32,000	63,685	31,685
170,000	34,000	68,385	34,385
180,000	36,000	73,085	37,085
190,000	38,000	77,785	39,785
200,000	40,000	82,485	42,485
210,000	42,000	87,185	45,185
220,000	44,000	91,885	47,885
230,000	46,000	96,585	50,585
240,000	48,000	101,285	53,285
250,000	50,000	105,985	55,985
260,000	52,000	110,685	58,685
270,000	54,000	115,385	61,385
280,000	56,000	120,085	64,085
290,000	58,000	124,785	66,785
300,000	60,000	129,485	69,485

When profits reach £100,000 sole traders start losing their income tax personal allowance and when profits reach £120,000 the personal allowance will have already completely disappeared. At this point a company will be paying over £22,000 less tax than a sole trader.

When profits reach £150,000 sole traders face their final attack from the taxman, becoming 'super rate' taxpayers who pay tax at 47%. By the time profits reach £200,000 this tax rate will have taken its toll and the company (still paying tax at 20%) will be paying £42,485 less tax than the sole trader.

If we bump the profits right up to £300,000, the company pays £69,485 less tax than the sole trader!

Table 1 compares corporation tax and self-employment tax at lots of different profit levels.

You may be able to spot that the tax savings become *proportionately* larger as profits increase. The reason for this is that companies with profits below £300,000 pay tax at a flat rate of 20% – the tax rate does not increase as the amount of profit increases.

Most tax systems in the Western world are *progressive* – in other words, tax rates go up as income goes up. But in the UK, a company with £300,000 of profits pays tax at the same rate as a company with £1,000 of profits.

What more incentive do you need to grow your business?

Profits Below £30,000 – Should I Use a Company?

Table 1 does not necessarily imply that businesses with profits under £30,000 should avoid using a company.

What I am attempting to do in these early chapters is slowly build a picture of how company owners and sole traders are taxed. The table doesn't look at the whole picture.

For example, we haven't included the fact that company owners can extract tax-free salaries that are also tax deductible for the company and therefore reduce the company's tax bill.

For now all we can say is that: Corporation tax bills can be a lot lower than self-employed tax bills but not at all profit levels.

The overall effective tax rate of a sole trader goes higher and higher as profits increase. For example, a sole trader earning £50,000 of profits only pays tax at an overall rate of about 26%; a sole trader earning £200,000 pays tax at an overall rate of 41%.

The important thing to note is that:

As profits go up, using a company becomes more and more attractive.

However, as mentioned already, we are not looking at the complete picture yet. Two things we have ignored are:

- Business owners with income from other sources

- The tax paid by the *owners* of the company when they extract income

Business Owners with Other Income

If you have income from other sources the self-employed tax bills listed in Table 1 may be too low.

For example, let's say you already own some properties that produce rental income and then decide to start a new business venture.

If you set up a company to house the new business you will pay 20% corporation tax on the profits. However, if you operate as a sole trader you may end up paying 20% or 40% income tax on your profits if your rental income is already using up your income tax personal allowance and some or all of your basic-rate band. You may also end up paying 9% national insurance as well.

The bottom line: a company may be an excellent tax shelter if you have existing income from other sources and do not need to extract income from the company initially.

Profit Extraction = Additional Tax?

For sole traders and partnerships there is no further tax to worry about once income tax and national insurance have been paid on the profits of the business. In other words, the numbers in Table 1 generally tell us the whole picture.

However, if company owners want to get their hands on the company's profits they have to pay themselves a salary or dividend. This could result in less tax or more tax being paid.

For example, if a company owner can pay himself a small tax-free salary that is also a tax-deductible expense for the company, this will lower the total tax payable, thus making using a company more attractive, especially at lower profit levels.

However, if the company owner wants to extract more income (usually dividends) there may be additional income tax to pay and this could increase the total tax bill, thereby making using a company less attractive.

The critical question is: After paying any extra tax, are you still better off using a company? Answering this very important question is the main focus of this guide.

Reinvesting Profits

Although extra tax is often payable when profits are withdrawn from a company via a salary or dividend, no extra tax has to be paid if profits are simply *reinvested*.

So the next important point to note is that:

Using a company is attractive if profits are reinvested.

Reinvesting profits may allow you to create a more valuable business that generates even higher income or can be sold for a significant sum at some point in the future.

Selling businesses is probably the most tax-efficient way to make a living in the UK. The proceeds are subject to capital gains tax and, if your company is a 'trading' company (rather than an investment company), you may qualify for Entrepreneurs' Relief.

Entrepreneurs Relief allows up to £10 million of capital gains from the sale of businesses during your lifetime to be taxed at just 10%. The relief applies on a per person basis, so couples can have up to £20 million of gains taxed at 10%.

In effect, selling a business is a way of converting fully taxed income (future profits, salary, dividends etc) into capital gains that are taxed at a much lower rate.

Even if you decide not to sell your business, reinvesting profits will allow you to earn a higher income in the future, if done wisely.

Again using a company will add a great deal more powder to your keg. A company with £100,000 of profits will have around £14,000 more money left after tax than a sole trader. This money can then be spent on computers or developing new products etc.

A company with £200,000 profits will have over £42,000 more money left after tax.

Of course, it's very unlikely that all of the profits of your business can be reinvested. If you want to pay yourself some income the incorporation question becomes a great deal more complex.

A whole host of factors come into play: how much of the company's profit you want to extract each year, whether to pay yourself a salary or dividends, the level of the company's profits and the tax-splitting opportunities available to you and your spouse or partner.

We will take a look at each of these factors in the chapters that follow.

Part 3

How Company Owners Can Pay Less Tax

Chapter 9

Employment Income

When HMRC and tax professionals talk about 'employment income', they are referring to salaries and bonuses.

These are subject to income tax and national insurance. They are also generally a tax-deductible expense for the company (i.e. they reduce the company's corporation tax bill).

Company owners pay the same income tax on their salaries as self-employed business owners (see Chapter 7). However the national insurance position is different: company owners pay 12% on earnings between £7,956 and £41,865 (sole traders pay 9%).

Combined Tax Rates

As a result, the combined marginal rates of income tax and national insurance applying to salaries in 2014/15 are as follows:

Income up to £7,956	0%
Income from £7,956 to £10,000	12%
Income from £10,000 to £41,865	32%
Income from £41,865 to £100,000	42%
Income from £100,000 to £120,000	62%
Income from £120,000 to £150,000	42%
Income over £150,000	47%

Employer's National Insurance

There isn't a huge amount of difference between the tax paid by sole traders and the tax paid by company owners themselves on their salaries. However, we haven't looked at the BIG tax blow of paying salaries yet: Employer's national insurance!

Most employees don't lose much sleep over their employer's national insurance bill. However, as a company owner, the company's money is effectively your money so this extra tax is an important consideration.

Companies currently pay class 1A national insurance at 13.8% on every single pound of salary the director earns over £7,956.

Employer's national insurance is, however, a tax-deductible expense for corporation tax purposes.

There is also a new 'employment allowance' which reduces the national insurance paid by most companies by £2,000 per year. We'll return to this at the end of the chapter.

So what has all this got to do with the decision to start a company? If you start a company and take all your income as salary, you could end up paying a lot more tax than a sole trader.

Example

Margo is a sole trader with profits of £50,000 in 2014/15. We know from Table 1 that her total tax bill comes to £12,985, leaving her with an after-tax income of £37,015.

Richard owns a company that also makes profits of £50,000 (before deducting his salary and employers national insurance on that salary). Richard decides to extract all of the company's profits as salary. He doesn't pay himself £50,000 because he wants to leave enough money in the company to pay the employer's national insurance on his salary.

He decides to pay himself a salary of £44,902. The employer's national insurance comes to £5,098 – total cost £50,000. The company doesn't have any corporation tax to pay because the salary and employer's national insurance reduce its taxable profits to zero.

Richard himself will pay income tax of £7,588 and employee's national insurance of £4,130, leaving him with an after-tax income of £33,184.

In summary, the sole trader's total tax bill is £12,985. The company owner's total tax bill is £16,816 (including employer's national insurance). The company owner pays £3,831 more tax than the sole trader.

Table 2 shows the total tax paid by sole traders and company owners at different profit levels. In each case the company owner extracts all of the company's profits as salary. At all profit levels the company owner pays more tax than the sole trader.

TABLE 2
Company Owner vs Sole Trader Tax 2014/15
All Company Profits Taken as Salary

Profits £	Company Owner £	Sole Trader £	Tax Loss £
10,000	463	327	136
20,000	4,438	3,227	1,211
30,000	8,463	6,127	2,336
40,000	12,488	9,027	3,461
50,000	16,816	12,985	3,831
60,000	21,719	17,185	4,535
70,000	26,623	21,385	5,238
80,000	31,526	25,585	5,941
90,000	36,429	29,785	6,645
100,000	41,333	33,985	7,348
110,000	46,236	40,185	6,051
120,000	52,422	46,385	6,037
130,000	59,083	50,585	8,498
140,000	64,946	54,785	10,161
150,000	69,849	58,985	10,865
160,000	74,753	63,685	11,068
170,000	79,673	68,385	11,289
180,000	85,016	73,085	11,932
190,000	90,359	77,785	12,574
200,000	95,702	82,485	13,217
210,000	101,044	87,185	13,860
220,000	106,387	91,885	14,502
230,000	111,730	96,585	15,145
240,000	117,072	101,285	15,788
250,000	122,415	105,985	16,431
260,000	127,758	110,685	17,073
270,000	133,101	115,385	17,716
280,000	138,443	120,085	18,359
290,000	143,786	124,785	19,001
300,000	149,129	129,485	19,644

What Table 2 tells us is that if you run your business via a company, and take all your income as salary, you will not save any tax. In fact it could be a complete disaster. Your total tax bill could increase by thousands of pounds!

Although sole traders and company owners are subject to the same income tax rates on their earnings, they are subject to completely different national insurance systems.

This leads us to conclude that:

Using a company is a bad idea when all income is taken as salary.

Fortunately, as a company owner you do not have to take all your income as salary. You may be able to pay yourself dividends.

The key thing to remember is that national insurance is a tax on 'earned' income. A salary is earned income – it rewards your hard work. Dividends, on the other hand, are not earned income – they reward your entrepreneurship. So salaries, bonuses and the like fall into the national insurance net, dividend payments do not.

As we shall see in the chapters that follow, if you take some of your income as dividends you may be able to save thousands of pounds in tax by running your business via a company.

We will explain how dividends are taxed in the next chapter.

£2,000 Employment Allowance

Most business tax cuts in recent times (eg cuts in corporation tax and increases in the annual investment allowance) have only helped big businesses. This one helps small ones too.

Most businesses now receive an employment allowance of £2,000 per year to offset against their national insurance bills. In other words, if your business would normally pay £10,000 of employer's national insurance, it will now pay just £8,000.

Where a company has no other employees (or perhaps just a few low-paid employees), the employment allowance will reduce the national insurance payable on the directors' own salaries.

For example, a company with no employees and only one director can pay that director a salary of up to £22,449 with no employer's national insurance.

A company with no employees and two directors (e.g. a husband and wife) can pay the directors a salary of up to £15,202 each with no employer's national insurance.

However, even with the £2,000 national insurance rebate, most sole traders will still pay less tax than company owners who withdraw all the profits as salary.

Furthermore, the employment allowance will not reduce the tax on the director's own salary if it is used up paying salaries to other people.

Chapter 10

Using Dividends to Escape Tax

Company owners can avoid large national insurance bills by paying themselves dividends.

The important thing to note is that dividends are paid out of *profits*. If your company doesn't have any profits, it cannot pay you dividends.

Also, dividends are not a tax-deductible expense for the business. In other words, dividends are paid out of profits that have already been subjected to corporation tax. Salaries and bonuses, on the other hand, are tax-deductible expenses.

Remember, as a company owner, you should be concerned about both your tax bill *and* the company's tax bill. So the fact that the company can claim salaries as a tax deduction, but not dividends, is something that should be borne in mind when you structure your pay. We'll return to this later.

First of all let's examine how dividends are taxed.

How Dividends Are Taxed

Because dividends are paid out of profits that have already been taxed in the hands of the company, the income tax rates on dividends are lower than income tax rates on other types of income.

The income tax rates applying to *cash dividends* are:

- Basic-rate taxpayers   0%
- Higher-rate taxpayers   25%
- Additional rate taxpayers   30.6%

By cash dividends we mean the actual payment from the company to the director/shareholder.

Gross Dividends vs Cash Dividends

You are a higher-rate taxpayer if your income exceeds £41,865 in 2014/15. And if your income exceeds £150,000 you are an additional-rate taxpayer. However, those thresholds are for *gross* dividends, not the actual *cash* dividends you receive from the company.

Whereas company owners are mostly interested in their cash dividends (the money they actually withdraw from their companies), most tax calculations work with gross dividends.

Gross dividends are found by dividing cash dividends by 0.9:

Gross dividends = Cash dividends/0.9

For example, if you pay yourself a cash dividend of £90, the gross dividend is £100 (£90/0.9). The £10 difference is what's known as the dividend tax credit.

Gross dividends are taxed at the following rates:

- Basic-rate taxpayers   10%
- Higher-rate taxpayers   32.5%
- Additional rate taxpayers   37.5%

To calculate the final income tax bill you subtract the 10% dividend tax credit. The dividend tax credit is supposed to compensate company owners for the fact that dividends are paid out of profits that have already been subjected to corporation tax.

The effective income tax rates on gross dividends are as follows:

- Basic-rate taxpayers   0%
- Higher-rate taxpayers   22.5%
- Additional rate taxpayers   27.5%

It's all unnecessarily complicated – a bit like climbing over a mountain instead of walking around the side – but UK tax law carries a lot of baggage like this from years gone by. However, you do have to understand how dividends are taxed if you want to minimise the income tax payable on them!

The taxation of dividends is best illustrated with some examples:

Example 1

Bob Limited makes a profit of £20,000. After paying corporation tax at 20% the company is left with after-tax profits of £16,000. Bob, the company's owner, pays himself a cash dividend of £16,000 (a gross dividend of £17,778). He has no other taxable income.

Because Bob is a basic-rate taxpayer (his gross dividends are less than £41,865) he doesn't pay any income tax and is left with an after-tax income of £16,000.

Example 2

Bob Limited makes a profit of £60,000. After paying corporation tax at 20% the company is left with after-tax profits of £48,000. Bob, the company's owner, pays himself a cash dividend of £48,000 (a gross dividend of £53,333). He has no other taxable income.

The first £41,865 of Bob's gross dividend is tax free. The remaining £11,468 is taxed at an effective rate of 22.5%, resulting in an income tax bill of £2,580. Bob is left with an after-tax income of £45,420 (£48,000 cash dividend less £2,580 income tax).

Example 3

Bob Limited makes a profit of £200,000. After paying corporation tax at 20% the company is left with after-tax profits of £160,000. Bob, the company's owner, pays himself a cash dividend of £160,000 (a gross dividend of £177,778). He has no other taxable income.

Because Bob's income exceeds £120,000 his income tax personal allowance is taken away completely (see Chapter 7). And because his income exceeds £150,000 he is also an additional rate taxpayer. Consequently, the first £31,865 of his gross dividend is tax free (the basic-rate band for the current tax year), the next £118,135 is taxed at 22.5% and the final £27,778 is taxed at 27.5%.

The total tax bill is £34,219 and Bob is left with an after-tax income of £125,781 (£160,000 cash dividend less £34,219 income tax).

Company vs Sole Trader:
All Income Taken as Dividends

The important question is: Will a company owner who takes dividends pay less tax than a sole trader?

Table 3 shows the total tax (corporation tax and income tax) payable by a company owner who takes all of his income as dividends. It also shows the total tax (income tax and national insurance) payable by a sole trader.

At most profit levels the company owner pays less tax than the sole trader. However, while the tax savings are respectable, they are not huge.

For example, a business owner with profits of £50,000 can save £2,404 by using a company, a business owner with profits of £100,000 can save £3,404 in tax and a business owner with profits of £200,000 can save £8,265 in tax.

On average, the company owner gets to keep an extra 3% of the profits of the business

The main reason for the tax savings is national insurance: national insurance is payable on a sole trader's profits but company dividends are exempt.

However, the savings are not as big as they could be. If a company owner takes all of his income as dividends the total tax will always be *at least* 20%. This is because dividends are always paid out of company profits after paying corporation tax.

By contrast, some of a sole trader's profits are completely tax free thanks to the income tax personal allowance and national insurance threshold.

This explains why sole traders pay less tax than company owners when profits are quite small (below roughly £29,000).

Fortunately, company owners can also benefit from these tax-free allowances, as we shall see in the next chapter.

TABLE 3
Company Tax vs Sole Trader Tax 2014/15
All Company Profits Taken as Dividends

Profits £	Company £	Sole Trader £	Saving £
10,000	2,000	327	-1,673
20,000	4,000	3,227	-773
30,000	6,000	6,127	127
40,000	8,000	9,027	1,027
50,000	10,580	12,985	2,404
60,000	14,580	17,185	2,604
70,000	18,580	21,385	2,804
80,000	22,580	25,585	3,004
90,000	26,580	29,785	3,204
100,000	30,580	33,985	3,404
110,000	34,580	40,185	5,604
120,000	39,330	46,385	7,054
130,000	44,330	50,585	6,254
140,000	48,830	54,785	5,954
150,000	52,830	58,985	6,154
160,000	56,830	63,685	6,854
170,000	60,886	68,385	7,499
180,000	65,330	73,085	7,754
190,000	69,775	77,785	8,010
200,000	74,219	82,485	8,265
210,000	78,664	87,185	8,521
220,000	83,108	91,885	8,776
230,000	87,553	96,585	9,032
240,000	91,997	101,285	9,287
250,000	96,441	105,985	9,543
260,000	100,886	110,685	9,799
270,000	105,330	115,385	10,054
280,000	109,775	120,085	10,310
290,000	114,219	124,785	10,565
300,000	118,664	129,485	10,821

Chapter 11

Company Owners: Tax-free Salaries

So far we've shown that company owners pay more tax than sole traders when all income is taken as salary.

We've also shown that company owners generally pay less tax than sole traders when all income is taken as dividends.

In this chapter we will show how company owners can increase their tax savings by paying themselves a small salary as well as dividends.

Assumption: No Other Taxable Income

We will assume the company owner has no other taxable income. This keeps the number crunching as simple as possible.

It's not a totally unrealistic assumption either. Although most company owners have at least some other taxable income, for example some bank account interest or stock market dividends, many have no more than a few hundred pounds.

For those company owners with significant amounts of taxable income from other sources, for example rental profits from a portfolio of properties, an even smaller salary may be more tax efficient, as long as this does not jeopardize their state pension entitlement (see Chapter 12).

Why a Small Salary Is Tax Efficient

The first few thousand pounds of either salary or dividends are tax-free in the hands of the company owner, if the payments fall below the various income tax and national insurance thresholds.

However, a dividend payment is not necessarily tax efficient for the company (and, of course, most company owners are equally concerned about their company's tax position as their own personal tax position).

Dividends are paid out of a company's after-tax profits, i.e. after corporation tax has been paid. So every dividend has a corporation tax bill attached to it.

A salary, on the other hand, is a tax deductible expense for the company. Salaries are subject to employer's national insurance but this only kicks in when the salary exceeds £7,956. Salaries below this threshold have no national insurance consequences.

In summary, a small salary is generally much more tax efficient than a dividend. Not only is it tax free in the hands of the company owner (assuming he has no other taxable income), it provides a corporation tax saving for the company as well.

This corporation tax saving is essentially a cashback for the company and is why the company owner should consider paying a salary, even if the money isn't needed.

For the same reason, the company owner should consider paying salaries to their spouse or partner and children, including their minor children, wherever possible.

How Much Salary?
Companies with Employees
(i.e. with no spare employment allowance)

We will assume that the company's £2,000 national insurance employment allowance is already used up paying salaries to other employees, i.e. there is no spare employment allowance for the directors own salaries.

We will also assume that the company pays 20% corporation tax.

So how much salary should a company owner in this situation take? There are two important income tax and national insurance thresholds for the current 2014/15 tax year:

- National insurance   £7,956
- Income tax   £10,000

For the 2014/15 tax year the most tax efficient salary for directors of companies with no spare employment allowance is £7,956. This will not attract any employee's or employer's national insurance and, providing the company owner has no other income, it will also be free from income tax.

Because salaries are usually a tax deductible expense, a salary of £7,956 will also save the company £1,591 in corporation tax:

£7,956 x 20% corporation tax = £1,591

Salary of £10,000?

Why not increase the salary from £7,956 to £10,000 to use up the company owner's income tax personal allowance? Because the extra £2,044 of salary will attract both employee's and employer's national insurance, at 12% and 13.8% respectively:

Extra national insurance

£2,044 x 12%	£245
£2,044 x 13.8%	£282
Total	£527

On the plus side, the extra salary and employer's national insurance will attract corporation tax relief at 20%:

Extra corporation tax relief

£2,044 x 20%	£409
£282 x 20%	£56
Total	£465

However, the extra national insurance outweighs the extra corporation tax relief, so further salary beyond £7,956 is not, strictly speaking, 'optimal' (although there may be other reasons why a higher salary is desirable). The extra tax cost is not significant (around £60), so whether you take a salary of £7,956, £10,000, or something in between, probably won't make a huge amount of difference at the end of the day.

How Much Salary?
Companies with No Employees
(i.e. with spare employment allowance)

If the company does not use up its £2,000 employment allowance paying salaries to other employees, there will be spare employment allowance for the directors own salaries.

Directors of these companies can pay themselves salaries of more than £7,956 without having to worry about *employer's* national insurance.

The question is, should they?

If a company owner increases his salary from £7,956 to £10,000 no national insurance will be paid by the company itself but the extra salary will result in a national insurance bill of £245 for the director personally (£2,044 x 12%). That's the bad news.

The good news is that, by increasing the director's salary from £7,956 to £10,000, at least £409 of additional corporation tax relief is obtained for the company (£2,044 x 20%).

The extra corporation tax relief outweighs the national insurance cost by £164 in the average small company.

In summary, for company owners with no employees (i.e. spare employment allowance), a salary of up to £10,000 will be more tax efficient than a salary of £7,956.

Is it worth paying a salary of more than £10,000? In most cases the answer is no because any additional salary will also be subject to income tax.

The 20% income tax and 12% national insurance paid by the director outweighs the 20% corporation tax relief enjoyed by the company.

Smaller or Higher Salaries

Although a salary of £7,956 or £10,000 may be 'optimal' for some company owners, a lower or higher salary may be preferable in some cases.

For example, even if the company has spare employment allowance, the directors may still decide to pay themselves a salary of £7,956 each to avoid the hassle of having to make any national insurance payments (for example, to avoid late payment penalties).

Although a salary of £7,956 is completely tax free, it still has to be reported to HMRC as part of the normal payroll process (although it may be possible to make a single annual payroll submission in some circumstances).

Where a company owner's taxable income exceeds £120,000 (i.e. he has no personal allowance), a small tax saving may be achieved by taking a salary smaller than £10,000 or £7,956.

A smaller salary may also be desirable when the director has income from other sources that uses up some or all of his income tax personal allowance.

However, taking a smaller salary may have other adverse consequences. For example, it may reduce your state pension entitlement.

There may also be tax and non-tax reasons why you may wish to pay yourself a salary *higher* than £7,956 or £10,000. Some company owners may wish to pay themselves a higher salary because, although strictly speaking not 'optimal', this lets them take a bigger chunk of income out of the company on a regular basis, without some of the hassle that comes with paying dividends (for example, making sure the company has sufficient distributable profits and that dividends are properly declared).

Summary

In all the examples that follow in which we compare the tax paid by self-employed business owners and company owners, we will assume, for better or worse, that the company owner takes a salary of £7,956 and the rest of his income as dividends.

Although a higher or lower salary may be 'optimal' or desirable in certain circumstances, the additional savings are usually quite small.

In other words, using £7,956 is probably perfectly adequate when it comes to examining the tax savings that can be achieved by using a company.

Chapter 12

Salaries: Pension Benefits

Apart from being tax efficient a salary confers two extra benefits on company owners:

- State pension entitlement
- Ability to make private pension contributions

State Pension Entitlement

To protect your state pension entitlement you should pay yourself a salary that is greater than the national insurance 'lower earnings limit'.

For 2014/15, the lower earnings limit is £111 per week which requires a total annual salary of at least £5,772.

If you want to protect your state pension entitlement, a salary of at least £5,772 should be paid in 2014/15 in preference to taking dividends.

Private Pension Contributions

Everyone under the age of 75 can make a pension contribution of £3,600 per year. The actual cash contribution would be £2,880, with the taxman adding £720 to bring the total gross contribution to £3,600.

If you want to make bigger pension contributions the contributions you make *personally* (as opposed to contributions made by your company) must not exceed your 'relevant UK earnings'. Salaries count as earnings, dividends do not.

For a small company director taking a tax-free salary of £7,956, the maximum pension contribution that can be made is £7,956.

This is the maximum *gross* contribution. The director would personally invest £6,365 (£7,956 x 0.8) and the taxman will top this up with £1,591 of basic-rate tax relief for a gross contribution of £7,956.

Directors who want to make bigger pension contributions have two choices:

- Pay themselves a bigger salary (ie more earnings)
- Get the company to make the pension contributions

Company pension contributions are certainly very tax efficient, as they generally provide corporation tax relief for the company and also avoid national insurance.

It is possible that HM Revenue & Customs will deny the company tax relief if the pension contribution, together with the director/shareholder's other remuneration, amounts to more than a commercial rate of pay for the job they do for the company.

This problem is fairly rare in practice but could affect any company owner who does not play a fully active role in the day-to-day management of their business.

Chapter 13

Company vs Sole Trader: The Final Outcome

In the previous two chapters we explained why many company owners can benefit from taking a small tax-free salary.

In this chapter we'll compare the total tax paid by sole traders and company owners when the company owner pays himself a salary of £7,956 and extracts the remaining profits as dividends.

Then in Chapter 14 and Part 5 we'll see how company owners can save even more tax by:

- Reinvesting some profits

- Involving a spouse/partner in the business

Table 4 compares the total tax (corporation tax and income tax) payable by a company owner with the total tax (income tax and national insurance) payable by a sole trader.

At almost all profit levels the company owner pays less tax than the sole trader. For example, a business owner with profits of £60,000 will save £3,996 in tax by using a company, a business owner with profits of £120,000 will save £8,001 in tax and a business owner with profits of £300,000 will save £10,578 in tax.

On average, the company owner gets to keep an extra 5% of the profits of the business, i.e. his overall tax rate is five percentage points lower.

Remember this is the *annual saving* – it may be possible to enjoy similar savings every year.

However, when profits are modest, a company will not produce meaningful tax savings. For example, when profits are £10,000 you will end up paying more tax (£82) by using a company and when profits are £20,000 you will save just £818 in tax.

TABLE 4
Company Owner vs Sole Trader Tax 2014/15
Profits Taken as £7,956 Salary & Dividends

Profits £	Company Owner £	Sole Trader £	Saving £
10,000	409	327	-82
20,000	2,409	3,227	818
30,000	4,409	6,127	1,718
40,000	6,409	9,027	2,618
50,000	9,188	12,985	3,796
60,000	13,188	17,185	3,996
70,000	17,188	21,385	4,196
80,000	21,188	25,585	4,396
90,000	25,188	29,785	4,596
100,000	29,188	33,985	4,796
110,000	33,188	40,185	6,996
120,000	38,384	46,385	8,001
130,000	44,273	50,585	6,312
140,000	49,029	54,785	5,755
150,000	53,029	58,985	5,955
160,000	57,029	63,685	6,655
170,000	61,129	68,385	7,255
180,000	65,573	73,085	7,511
190,000	70,018	77,785	7,767
200,000	74,462	82,485	8,022
210,000	78,907	87,185	8,278
220,000	83,351	91,885	8,533
230,000	87,796	96,585	8,789
240,000	92,240	101,285	9,044
250,000	96,685	105,985	9,300
260,000	101,129	110,685	9,555
270,000	105,573	115,385	9,811
280,000	110,018	120,085	10,067
290,000	114,462	124,785	10,322
300,000	118,907	129,485	10,578

How the Tax Savings Are Calculated

Taking a sample profit figure from Table 4 – £60,000 – let's examine how the numbers are calculated:

Sole Trader Tax Calculation

Income tax:	£
Profits	60,000
Less: Personal allowance	10,000
Taxable profits	50,000
£31,865 @ 20%	6,373
£18,135 @ 40%	7,254
Total	13,627
National insurance:	
Class 2	143
Class 4:	
£41,865 - £7,956 @ 9%	3,052
£60,000 - £41,865 @ 2%	363
Total	3,558

Total income tax and national insurance: £17,185

Company Tax Calculation

Corporation tax:	£
Profits	60,000
Less: salary	7,956
Taxable profits	52,044
Corporation tax @ 20%	10,409
After-tax profits	41,635
Income tax on dividend:	
Cash dividend	41,635
Gross dividend (£41,635/0.9)	46,261
Tax-free (£41,865 - £7,956)	33,909
Taxed @ 22.5% (£46,261 - £33,909)	12,352
Income tax	2,779

Total corporation tax and income tax: £13,188

Let's take another profit figure from Table 4 – £200,000 – and examine a slightly more complicated calculation:

Sole Trader Tax Calculation

Income tax:	£
Profits	200,000
Less: Personal allowance	0
Taxable profits	200,000
£31,865 @ 20%	6,373
£118,135 @ 40%	47,254
£50,000 @ 45%	22,500
Total	76,127
National insurance:	
Class 2	143
Class 4:	
£41,865 - £7,956 @ 9%	3,052
£200,000 - £41,865 @ 2%	3,163
Total	6,358

Total income tax and national insurance: £82,485

Company Tax Calculation

Corporation tax:	£
Profits	200,000
Less: salary	7,956
Taxable profits	192,044
Corporation tax @ 20%	38,409
After-tax profits	153,635
Taxable income:	
Salary	7,956
Gross dividend (£153,635/0.9)	170,706
Less: Personal allowance	0
Taxable income	178,662

Income tax on salary:
£7,956 x 20%   1,591

Income tax on dividend:
Tax-free dividend:
£31,865 - £7,956 = £23,909

Taxed @ 22.5%:
£150,000 - £31,865 = £118,135   26,580

Taxed @ 27.5%:
£178,662 - £150,000 = £28,662   7,882

Income tax   36,053

Total corporation tax and income tax: £74,462

If you compare the tax paid by the company owner in Table 4 above with the tax paid by the company owner in Table 3 (all profits extracted as dividends) you will see that taking a small salary reduces the company owner's tax bill by a further £1,591 or £1,392 when profits are between £10,000 and £110,000.

However, when profits exceed £120,000 the company owner starts to lose his income tax personal allowance and taking a salary (instead of taking all income as dividends) actually increases the total tax bill slightly. However, the additional tax cost is not significant (approximately £200) and, as explained in Chapter 12, the company owner may wish to continue receiving a salary to protect his state pension.

Other Company Tax Benefits & Drawbacks

While Table 4 is interesting it does not incorporate all of the tax benefits and drawbacks of using a company – that would be impossible.

In Part 7 we move beyond a strict comparison of tax rates and look at some of the other tax benefits and drawbacks of being a company owner or sole trader.

Keeping Money in the Company

So far, in all of the comparisons of company owners and sole traders we have assumed that the company owner takes all of the profits out of the business.

However, many company owners keep some profits in the company for two reasons:

- To avoid extortionate income tax rates
- To reinvest and grow the business

This is where companies really show their mettle and can produce significant tax savings.

In Part 6 we will see how company owners can alter the amount of income they extract and avoid various income thresholds where extortionate tax rates apply (sole traders cannot do this).

In the next chapter we take a look at how company owners who reinvest some of their profits often have a lot more financial firepower than sole traders.

Chapter 14

Reinvesting Profits to Make Bigger Tax Savings

Company owners have a lot more flexibility than sole traders: The profits of the business can either be kept inside the company or extracted as income.

This is one of the key tax benefits of using a company. Only corporation tax is payable on profits that are retained in the company. The company owners do not have to pay any additional income tax.

By contrast, sole traders pay income tax and national insurance on ALL their profits, irrespective of whether they are retained within the business or taken out as drawings.

Table 5 compares the total tax (corporation tax and income tax) payable by a company owner with the total tax (income tax and national insurance) payable by a sole trader. Again we assume that the company owner takes a salary of £7,956 and takes the rest of his income as dividends.

The difference between this table and Table 4 from the previous chapter is that the company owner only extracts 50% of the after-tax profits by way of dividend. The remaining profits are kept inside the company to fund future growth of the business.

The total tax bills shown in Table 5 speak for themselves: when a business is growing and using retained earnings as a source of finance, using a company can produce big tax savings.

For example, a business owner with profits of £60,000 will save £6,776 in tax by using a company, a business owner with profits of £80,000 will save £11,176 in tax and a business owner with profits of £120,000 will save £20,401 in tax.

On average, the company owner gets to keep an extra 14% of the profits of the business! Remember this is the *annual saving* – it may be possible to enjoy similar savings every year.

TABLE 5
Total Tax Bills Compared
50% Profit Reinvested

Profits £	Company £	Sole Trader £	Saving £
10,000	409	327	-82
20,000	2,409	3,227	818
30,000	4,409	6,127	1,718
40,000	6,409	9,027	2,618
50,000	8,409	12,985	4,576
60,000	10,409	17,185	6,776
70,000	12,409	21,385	8,976
80,000	14,409	25,585	11,176
90,000	16,984	29,785	12,801
100,000	19,984	33,985	14,001
110,000	22,984	40,185	17,201
120,000	25,984	46,385	20,401
130,000	28,984	50,585	21,601
140,000	31,984	54,785	22,801
150,000	34,984	58,985	24,001
160,000	37,984	63,685	25,701
170,000	40,984	68,385	27,401
180,000	43,984	73,085	29,101
190,000	46,984	77,785	30,801
200,000	49,984	82,485	32,501
210,000	52,984	87,185	34,201
220,000	56,231	91,885	35,654
230,000	59,986	96,585	36,598
240,000	63,931	101,285	37,354
250,000	67,875	105,985	38,109
260,000	71,820	110,685	38,865
270,000	74,825	115,385	40,560
280,000	77,825	120,085	42,260
290,000	80,825	124,785	43,960
300,000	83,825	129,485	45,660

How the Tax Savings Are Calculated

Taking a sample profit figure from Table 5 – £100,000 – let's examine how the company tax numbers are calculated (the sole trader figures are the same as in all previous tables):

Company Tax Calculation

Corporation tax:	£
Profits	100,000
Less: salary	7,956
Taxable profits	92,044
Corporation tax @ 20%	18,409
After-tax profits	73,635

After-tax profits:	£
Reinvested (73,635 x 50%)	36,818
Cash dividend	36,817

Income tax	
Gross dividend (36,817/0.9)	40,908
Tax-free (£41,865 - £7,956)	33,909
Taxed @ 22.5% (£40,908 - £33,909)	6,999
Income tax	1,575

Total corporation tax and income tax: £19,984

A sole trader who makes identical profits will pay £33,985 in tax.

Why are the tax savings so large for the company owner? For starters, he doesn't pay any national insurance, whereas the sole trader pays £4,358.

Second, despite making a profit of £100,000, the company owner doesn't pay much income tax because a lot of the profit is left inside the company.

Only £36,817 is paid out as a cash dividend (a gross dividend of £40,908) and most of this income is tax-free. Remember you only pay income tax on your dividends once you become a higher-rate taxpayer.

With a salary of £7,956 and gross dividend income of £40,908 the company owner's total taxable income is £48,864. Just £6,999 of this is taxable (£48,864 - £41,865 = £6,999), resulting in an income tax bill of £1,575 (£6,999 x 22.5%).

Even this £1,575 income tax bill is more than offset by the £1,591 corporation tax relief on the company owner's salary (£7,956 x 20% = £1,591).

All in all, the main tax payable by the company owner is corporation tax at a flat rate of 20% (which explains why the total tax on the £100,000 profit is almost exactly £20,000).

In contrast, the sole trader pays 40% income tax on a big chunk of his profit (£58,135), as well as national insurance and basic-rate income tax.

When Reinvesting Does Not Save Tax

If you compare the tax savings in Table 4 (all profits extracted) with the tax savings in Table 5 (50% of profits extracted) you will notice that reinvesting profits does not always produce additional tax savings for company owners.

More specifically, when profits are quite modest reinvesting produces no additional tax savings (i.e. the tax savings in Table 4 are identical to the savings in Table 5).

Reinvesting profits helps the company owner save *income tax* but company owners only pay income tax on their dividends if they are higher-rate taxpayers (i.e. if their income exceeds £41,865).

A company owner who takes a small salary of £7,956 and extracts all of the remaining after-tax profits as dividends will only start paying income tax when the pre-tax profits of the business exceed £46,104.

At lower profit levels the company owner will be a basic-rate taxpayer and will not pay any income tax on his dividends. Thus reinvesting profits when profits are below £46,104 will not generate any additional tax savings (although there may, of course, be other reasons why the company owner may wish to leave some of the profits in the company).

Maximising Tax-Free Income

In this chapter we've seen how company owners can increase their tax savings by reinvesting profits. Arguably, however, company owners should only reinvest profits once they've extracted the maximum amount of tax-free income from their companies.

A company owner can extract a tax-free income of £38,474 during the current 2014/15 tax year, made up of:

- Salary   £7,956
- Cash dividend   £30,518

A cash dividend of £30,518 is equivalent to a gross dividend of £33,909. Added to the £7,956 salary this produces a total income of £41,865 – the higher rate threshold.

If the company owner wants to extract bigger dividends he will start paying income tax.

A company owner may decide to not withdraw the maximum tax-free income for several reasons.

The decision to take a salary or dividend can be complex and should only be made after consulting a qualified accountant or tax adviser.

However, when it comes to tax-free income, it really is a case of use it or lose it: if you don't take the maximum tax-free amounts this year, you cannot take bigger tax-free amounts next year.

Danger of Holding Too Much Cash?

One reason why you should consider extracting cash from your company, even if this results in an income tax bill, is to reduce exposure to business risk.

Furthermore, if your company holds too many non-trading assets, including surplus cash, this may prejudice its status as a trading company. This means that you may not be able to, for example, claim Entrepreneurs Relief when the company is sold.

Cash may be treated as 'surplus' if you cannot show that it will be required by the business in the future. It may therefore be helpful to draw up a business plan showing how any cash balance will be used by the business.

However, provided the cash has been generated from trading activities and is not actively managed as an investment, holding large cash balances should not be considered a non-trading activity.

Part 4

Salaries & Dividends: Practical Issues & Dangers

Chapter 15

How to Avoid the National Minimum Wage

If you take a small salary from your company (for example, £7,956 or £10,000) there is a danger of falling foul of the national minimum wage regulations.

Where wages are too low, HMRC will force the company to make up the shortfall. Bigger wage payments may result in bigger national insurance bills for both the company and the director.

There is also a penalty equivalent to 100% of the unpaid wages with a maximum penalty of £20,000.

However, the key point to note about the national minimum wage is that it only applies to directors who have a contract of employment.

Due to the informal set up in many small companies, there may be some uncertainty as to whether an employment contract exists between the director and the company (employment contracts do not need to be in writing).

However, it is generally accepted amongst the tax profession that if you do not issue yourself with an explicit contract of employment the national minimum wage regulations will not apply.

This means you should be able to continue paying yourself a small salary, even if it is less than the national minimum wage.

However, risk averse company owners (those worried about potential penalties) should consider paying themselves enough salary to satisfy the national minimum wage regulations.

Directors with Contracts of Employment

If you do have a contract of employment the important point to note is that the national minimum wage does not apply to hours spent carrying out your duties as a director (or as a company secretary).

Of course, if you are involved full time in the management of your company the national minimum wage regulations will apply and you may need to pay yourself a bigger salary.

National Minimum Wage Rates

There are different levels of national minimum wage depending on your age. The main rate for those aged 21 and over is currently £6.31 per hour and will rise to £6.50 on 1 October 2014.

If you pay yourself a salary of £7,956 or £10,000 during 2014/15 this equates to around 24 to 30 hours per week of time spent actively managing the business.

If you spend, say, 35 hours per week actively managing your business, the total salary due for 2014/15 will be approximately £11,666:

35 x 52 weeks x £6.41* = £11,666

* Roughly the average minimum wage over the year

Fortunately this is not hugely higher than the optimal salary amounts but will still result in unwelcome national insurance charges.

The national insurance payable on this salary by the director would be £445 and £512 would be payable by the company (£0 if the company has spare employment allowance).

Of course, every case is different and some directors will be able to argue that they spend fewer hours actively managing the business.

Although it may seem that the best strategy is to simply not have a contract of employment, there may be other reasons why having such a contract is important.

Company Owners Who Aren't Directors

It is possible that some family members will be employees of the company but not directors. These individuals are subject to the national minimum wage for all hours spent working in the business (remember directors are exempt with respect to hours spent performing their duties as directors).

However, it is possible that if they only work part time, the salary that must be paid to them will still be within the optimal amounts of £7,956 or £10,000.

Chapter 16

Is My Salary Tax Deductible?

One of the benefits of getting your company to pay you a salary is that the amount will normally be a tax deductible expense and reduce the company's corporation tax bill.

However, it is important to point out that there is no automatic right to corporation tax relief. The amount paid has to be justified by the work carried out for the business and the individual's level of responsibility.

While this may not be an important issue for company owners who work full time in the business and pay themselves a small salary, it may be important if you start paying salaries to other family members, in particular those who only work on a part-time basis.

The question of whether your employment income will attract corporation tax relief may also become an issue if you decide to pay yourself a large one-off bonus.

Some of the factors that may determine whether a salary or bonus payment is tax deductible include:

- The number of hours worked in the business

- The individual's legal obligations and responsibilities (e.g. directors' duties)

- The amount of pay received by the company's other employees

- The pay received by employees at other companies performing similar roles

- The company's performance and ability to pay salaries/bonuses

In the case of large one-off bonus payments made only to the company's directors/shareholders it may be necessary to document the commercial rationale for the payment to show that the payment is justifiable. This can be done in the minutes of a directors' board meeting.

It may also be advisable to record the approval of any bonus in the minutes of a shareholders' meeting.

Chapter 17

Paying Salaries & Dividends: Practical Issues

Salaries – Payroll costs

Although a small salary is often tax efficient and protects your state pension entitlement, it may result in an additional payroll cost.

Since April 2013 employers have had to report salary payments to HMRC under the Real Time Information (RTI) regime. Under real time information, employers are required to submit a Full Payment Submission (FPS) to HMRC at the same time or before each payment is made to a director or employee.

The idea is to make sure the right amount of tax is paid at the right time. Under the previous system, employers generally only had to report payroll information to HMRC at the end of the year.

Under RTI the directors own salaries could result in additional payroll costs (for example, in small husband and wife companies or 'one man band' companies, where the only salaries paid are those of the directors themselves).

For example, if you pay yourself monthly and use an accountant to produce your payslips, you could end up paying anywhere between £200 and £400 per year in fees.

The additional cost of directors' salaries will be much lower if the business has other employees and already runs a payroll.

A small company that does not have other employees may be able to register as an annual payroll scheme with HMRC and pay salaries as a single annual lump sum (e.g. in March just before the end of the tax year).

With annual schemes an FPS is only expected in the month of payment and HMRC only has to be paid once a year. However, it is only possible to register as an annual scheme if all employees are paid annually at the same time.

Once a business is registered as an annual scheme, an Employer Payment Summary (EPS) is not required for the 11 months of the tax year where no payments are made to the directors. Schemes not registered as annual schemes have to make monthly submissions, even if no salaries are paid.

An additional problem may arise where directors withdraw cash from their companies and only later decide how these payments are to be treated (for example, as salaries or dividends).

Where the director's loan account is overdrawn, an amount withdrawn and subsequently designated as salary could result in a late filing penalty under RTI.

When directors withdraw money from their companies it is essential to decide up front the nature of the payment (e.g. salary, loan, dividend, reimbursement of expenses) and to have evidence supporting that decision.

For example, where a director borrows money from the company, the terms of the loan should be set out in writing. Withdrawals by directors that cannot be categorised might be treated as earnings by HMRC unless the company can prove otherwise.

Dividends – Distributable Profits

Distributable Profits

Under the Companies Act a company cannot legally pay a dividend unless it has sufficient distributable profits to cover it.

A company's distributable profits are its accumulated profits, less accumulated losses. This information can generally be found in the company's most recent annual accounts.

It is not necessary for the company to actually make a profit in the year the dividend is paid, as long as there are sufficient accumulated profits (after tax) from previous years.

If the distributable profits are not big enough to cover the dividend it may be necessary to prepare interim management accounts to justify the payment.

Before paying any dividends it is probably wise to speak to your accountant to check whether the company does indeed have sufficient distributable profits.

It may also be wise to check whether a loss has been realised since the last accounts were drawn up and whether any dividend will cause cash flow problems for the company.

In general, it is wise to be conservative and keep dividends to a reasonable level.

If the company does not have sufficient distributable profits to cover its dividend payments, the dividends will be illegal.

Illegal dividends have harmful tax and non-tax consequences. For example, the dividend may be treated as a loan which may result in the company having to pay a 25% 'section 455' tax charge.

Dividend Formalities & Paperwork

It is possible that HMRC will try to tax dividends as employment income. To help avoid any such challenge it is essential to ensure that dividends are properly declared and you have the supporting paperwork to prove it.

This includes:

- Holding a directors' board meeting to recommend the dividend payment (with printed minutes to prove the meeting took place)

- Holding a general meeting of the company's members (i.e. shareholders) to approve the dividend payment (with printed minutes to prove the meeting took place)

- Issuing a dividend voucher to each shareholder

Chapter 18

Dividends Taxed as Earnings

Recent tax cases demonstrate the potential danger that dividends paid to a director/shareholder may in some circumstances be vulnerable to a national insurance liability and possibly a full PAYE charge.

It remains to be seen how HMRC will choose to use these decisions in the context of family companies:

P A Holdings

PA Holdings switched from a conventional bonus arrangement to a more intricate structure whereby an employee benefit trust was funded by the company, which in turn awarded preference shares to employees. These preference shares duly paid a dividend after which they were redeemed.

The company and its employees argued that the dividends should be taxed as dividends using dividend tax rates and without any PAYE or national insurance implications.

By contrast, HMRC took the view that the dividends simply amounted to earnings and that the normal PAYE and national insurance payments should have been deducted from them and accounted for to HMRC.

The Court of Appeal overturned the decisions of the First Tier Tribunal and the Upper Tribunal and decided that the dividends were indeed earnings for employment and should therefore suffer deductions of income tax at source through PAYE. Both employers and employees national insurance deductions should also have been made.

PA Holdings initially decided to appeal to the Supreme Court but later threw in the towel. This led to fears that HMRC could attack company owners who take most of their income as dividends.

Many tax advisers argue that the aggressive tax planning undertaken by PA Holdings (trying to change bonuses into dividends for a large chunk of employees) is entirely different to the profit extraction model of most small companies.

In other words, most company owners should be able to continue paying themselves small salaries and taking the rest of their income as dividends with limited risk of challenge from HMRC.

Uniplex (UK) Ltd

Uniplex was sold a scheme aimed at giving employees dividend income instead of remuneration, issuing different classes of share to each employee. This type of arrangement is generally known as alphabet shares.

The scheme failed as it was not implemented as planned. However, the First Tier Tribunal judge added that the scheme, even if implemented correctly, might still have failed.

Stewart Fraser Ltd

This case involved a write off of loans by a close company to an employee shareholder. The loan write offs were treated as distributions taxable on the employee. HMRC successfully argued that national insurance liabilities were payable by the company on the loan write offs.

Practical Implications

The practical implications relate to the boundary between normal dividend payments and those which under the PA Holdings/Uniplex/Stewart Fraser case principles would be treated as employment earnings and hence attract income tax and national insurance deductions through PAYE. For instance in PA Holdings the First Tier Tribunal said:

"if something is paid out as a distribution by a company to an investing shareholder then the issue of derivation may arise if the shareholder is also an employee. The facts may show that the derivation of a dividend

from a share may not be related to earnings because the acquisition and ownership of the share was not related to earnings or more generally to the status of the individual as an employee of the company".

In Uniplex, the First Tier Tribunal said:

"The PA Holdings case is authority for the proposition that payments from a party other than the employer can be from an employee's employment" and *"It may well have still been the case that the full amount would have been taxable because employees had given no consideration for the payment other than their services".*

Summary

Dividends paid to an employee-shareholder may in some circumstances be vulnerable to a national insurance liability, and possibly to a full PAYE charge. It remains to be seen how HMRC will choose to use these decisions in the contexts of family companies and remuneration planning generally.

Chapter 19

Small Salary, Big Dividends: Potential Dangers

It is quite common practice for company owners to pay themselves a small salary and take the rest of their income as dividends. Many accountants have been recommending this strategy for years.

However, it is important to point out that some tax advisors are cautious about certain aspects of this tax planning technique, especially in light of recent court decisions like PA Holdings, where the Court of Appeal decided that certain dividends should be subject to PAYE and national insurance (see Chapter 18).

There is a fear that cases like this will create a wide precedent for any employer that pays dividends to its staff. It is difficult to quantify the potential danger, however, because a lot depends on HMRC's willingness to act. The most vulnerable, arguably, are those that use tax planning techniques that HMRC may view as aggressive, including possibly:

- Large scale contrived arrangements where dividends are created for tax avoidance purposes (as in PA Holdings).

- Directors' loans that are written off and taxed as dividends.

- Dividend waivers that are used to divert income to other shareholders, for example where a director waives his own dividends so that his wife can receive more tax-free income. HMRC recently succeeded in challenging dividend waivers in the case of *Donovan & McLaren v HMRC*.

- Certain 'Alphabet' share arrangements, where different classes of shares (A, B, C etc) have no substantive rights other than to dividends. These arrangements are often used to substitute dividends for bonuses.

- Situations where previous salaries have been reduced in favour of dividends.

The sixty-four thousand dollar question is: where does this leave the average small company owner taking a small salary and the rest of his income as dividends?

At the time of writing it would appear that most small companies are not under attack but this state of affairs could change at any time. The small salary/big dividend tax planning technique does not produce guaranteed tax savings. There is a danger, no matter how small, that HMRC may try to tax your dividends as earnings, if not now then at some point in the future.

Also, with regards to the last point in the above list, please note that some (more conservative) tax advisors argue that if you are currently taking a salary that is larger than the 'optimal' amounts outlined in Chapter 11 you should not reduce it.

There is also a danger that at some point in the future legislation could be introduced that imposes heavier tax on dividends from close companies. This could completely negate many of the tax benefits of running your business as a limited company.

Chapter 20

Personal Service Companies

If your company is classed as a personal service company, many of the tax-planning opportunities available to other company owners may not be available, for example the ability to take dividends that are free from national insurance.

Personal service companies have to operate the infamous 'IR35' regime which means the company may be forced to calculate a notional salary for the director/shareholder.

This deemed income will be subject to PAYE and national insurance.

Essentially, HMRC may ignore the company set up and treat most of the company's income as employment income.

Which Companies Are Affected by IR35?

This is where it all becomes a bit of a grey area (which is why professional advice is essential).

A personal service company is, generally speaking, a firm that receives all or most of its income from services provided by the director/shareholder.

Often the work will be carried out for just one client, often for a long period of time, and the client will probably only want the personal services of the company owner (hence IR35 often applies to 'one man band' companies).

Essentially HMRC is looking for cases of 'disguised employment'. In other words, ignoring the fact that there is an intermediary company, the relationship is more like an employer/employee relationship rather than the kind of relationship that exists between independent self-employed business owners and their clients.

Where such 'disguised employment' exists, the company must apply the IR35 regime to the payments received from that client – effectively treating most of those payments as if they were salary paid to the director/shareholder.

A typical situation that might be caught under the IR35 rules is where the individual resigns as an employee and then goes back to the same job but working through a company.

However, it's all very subjective, with a long line of legal cases adding to the confusion.

Personal service companies can be found in many different business sectors: the most cited example is IT consultants.

They also came under the media spotlight in recent times when it was disclosed that some BBC presenters were operating as 'freelancers' via personal service companies, when many would argue that they are in fact nothing but employees of the BBC.

Business Entity Tests

In May 2012 HMRC published a set of 'business entity tests' to help companies assess whether they should be applying the IR35 rules.

Essentially, the tests attempt to distinguish between companies that are truly independent businesses and those that are simply employment in another guise.

There are 12 tests with different points attached to each. By adding up the total points, you can assess which risk band you fall into:

Fewer than 10 points   High risk
10 to 20 points   Medium risk
More than 20 points   Low risk

The tests are as follows:

1. Business Premises Test. Does your business own or rent business premises that are separate both from your home and from the end client's premises? *Score 10 points if the answer is yes.*

2. PII Test. Do you need professional indemnity insurance? *Score 2 points if the answer is yes.*

3. Efficiency Test. Has your business had the opportunity in the last 24 months to increase its income by working more efficiently (e.g. contract clauses that pay you a fixed amount for a job even if you finish early)? *Score 10 points if the answer is yes.*

4. Assistance Test. Does your business engage any workers (other than the directors/shareholders) who bring in at least 25% of the yearly turnover? *Score 35 points if the answer is yes.*

5. Advertising Test. Has your business spent over £1,200 on advertising in the last 12 months? *Score 2 points if the answer is yes.*

6. Previous PAYE Test. Has the current client engaged you on PAYE employment terms within the 12 months that ended on the last 31 March, with no major changes to your working arrangements? *Score minus 15 points if answer is yes.*

7. Business Plan Test. Does your business have a business plan with a cash flow forecast that you update regularly? Does your business have a business bank account, identified as such by the bank, which is separate from your personal account? *Score 1 point if your answer to both questions is yes.*

8. Repair at Own Expense. Would your business have to bear the cost of having to put right any mistakes? *Score 4 points if your answer is yes.*

9. Client Risk Test. Has your business been unable to recover payment:
- For work done in the last 24 months?
- More than 10% of yearly turnover?

Score 10 points if your answer is yes.

10. Billing Test. Do you invoice for work carried out before being paid and negotiate payment terms? *Score 2 points if your answer is yes.*

11. Right of Substitution Test. Does your business have the right to send a substitute? *Score 2 points if your answer is yes.*

12. Actual Substitution Test. Have you hired anyone in the last 24 months to do the work you have taken on? *Score 20 points if the answer is yes.*

The business entity tests may help you work out the overall risk that IR35 applies and the likelihood of an HMRC enquiry. However, they do not tell you whether IR35 actually applies.

The tests look at how your business works overall in order to gauge the risk that HMRC will check whether IR35 applies to you. For the purposes of deciding if IR35 applies, you need to consider each engagement separately.

New HMRC Guidance

In June 2014 HMRC published new guidance which provides an overview of the intermediaries legislation and how to work out if IR35 applies.

The guidance can be downloaded here:

www.hmrc.gov.uk/ir35/intermediaries-legislation-ir35.pdf

Ultimately, however, professional advice will still be required to determine whether you are subject to IR35 or not.

Chapter 21

Future Tax Changes

In this guide we've seen how company owners can end up with lower tax bills than sole traders. However, it is very important to make this point:

The tax savings are not guaranteed or set in stone

The tax regime is constantly changing and it's possible that changes will be made that will make it less attractive to use a company – even if those changes only take place several years from now.

Increase in Corporation Tax Rates

It's unlikely that corporation tax will increase in the short term. On the contrary, the Coalition Government has been furiously cutting corporation tax rates in recent years.

In April 2015 the main rate will fall to 20% – it was 28% a few years ago! The Government also reversed Labour's attempt to increase the small companies rate from 21% to 22%. Instead George Osborne reduced it to 20%.

Verdict: an increase in corporation tax is highly unlikely while the current Government is in power. But who knows what could happen in the future.

Merger of Income Tax & National Insurance

In the March 2012 Budget the Chancellor reiterated the Government's desire to merge income tax and national insurance:

"We are also pressing forward with our ambition to integrate the operation of income tax and national insurance I announced at last year's Budget – so we don't ask businesses to run two different payroll tax administrations."

The Government seems to accept that national insurance is just tax by another name. It would be far more honest to have a 32% basic rate of income tax on earnings, instead of 20% income tax plus 12% national insurance.

However, such a change could not be introduced overnight. According to HM Treasury:

"The detailed and extensive work the Government has done so far shows that this is a large and complex reform. The Government also understands that employers are adjusting to a large number of tax reforms that have already been set out.

Nevertheless, there were press reports as recently as June 2014 that the Conservatives plan to press ahead with the merger of income tax and national insurance and possibly include this reform in their next general election manifesto. These rumours have apparently been denied by Downing Street.

Many are sceptical that such a radical reform of the tax system will take place at all. There would be winners but also losers and the coalition Government will probably not be able to afford creating more losers, following years of public spending cuts.

Writing in *The Times*, former Chancellor of the Exchequer Nigel Lawson, who investigated such a reform in the 1980s, warned George Osborne that merging the two taxes is a "huge elephant trap":

"A merger of the two would, in practice, be very costly and (because there would be both winners and losers) highly unpopular, all to little advantage. So I say to George: Don't go there."

Whether such a significant change to the tax system will take place remains to be seen. It is also difficult to ascertain how such a change would affect the tax paid by company owners on their salaries and dividends. Would the new merged tax only apply to earnings (i.e. salaries) or would dividends and other types of income also be taxed at higher rates?

All that can be said at this stage is that a merger of income tax and national insurance *could* result in company owners paying more tax on their income.

The General Anti-Abuse Rule

A new general anti-abuse rule (GAAR) came into operation on 17 July 2013.

Tax arrangements are "abusive" if they cannot reasonably be regarded as a reasonable course of action – this is commonly referred to as the double reasonableness test.

Clearly it's very subjective and HMRC has sought to reassure taxpayers that there will be a "high threshold" for showing that tax arrangements are abusive:

"There may be a range of views on whether any tax arrangements can be regarded as a reasonable course of action. It is possible that there could be both a reasonably held view that tax arrangements are reasonable and a reasonably held view that the same tax arrangements are unreasonable. In such circumstances the tax arrangements will not be abusive."

An indicator that tax arrangements may not be abusive is if they were "established practice" when entered into and HMRC indicated its acceptance of that practice at the time.

Tax arrangements may be abusive if, for example, the tax result is different to the 'economic' result, for example tax deductions or tax losses that are significantly greater than actual expenses or real economic losses.

If you think that all of the above is a bit vague and subjective, you are not alone. Even the best tax brains in the land don't know what this test means in practice. When legislation contains words like "reasonable" and "abusive" you know you have to be on your guard!

The question being asked by some tax advisers is this: will the anti-abuse rule be used to attack the sort of 'normal' or 'mainstream' tax planning carried out by thousands of small company owners, for example taking small salaries and dividends?

Many tax experts believe that well-established, conventional tax planning will not be attacked by HMRC using the GAAR. Instead the focus will be on the extreme end, for example 'aggressive' or 'artificial' tax avoidance schemes.

However, at present the simple truth is that no one knows how HMRC will apply the anti-abuse rule in practice and whether it will eventually affect many mainstream tax planning practices, including some of those contained in this guide.

Changes to Personal Circumstances

It's not just changes to tax laws that could undermine the tax savings you enjoy from using a company. Changes to your personal circumstances could have a similar effect.

For example, in Table 4 we saw that, at low profit levels, using a company does not save much tax.

In the worst-case scenario – if profits become losses – the company may have to start paying salaries instead of dividends (dividends require profits) and the company owner could face a significantly higher tax bill than a sole trader.

Part 5

How Couples Can Save Tax

Chapter 22

Companies Owned by Couples

So far we've compared the total tax paid by a sole trader with the total tax paid by a single company owner. But what if your spouse, common-law spouse or some other person is involved in the business?

In this chapter we compare the total tax paid by a *partnership* (two partners) with the total tax paid by two company owners. To start with we'll assume that the company owners pay themselves salaries of £7,956 each and extract all of the remaining profits as dividends. After that we'll find out how much extra tax can be saved by reinvesting profits.

Sole traders and partnerships are taxed in pretty much the same way: each partner pays income tax and national insurance on his share of the profits. We'll assume that each partner receives 50% of the profits.

Table 6 compares the total tax (corporation tax and income tax) payable by two company owners with the total tax (income tax and national insurance) payable by two business partners.

At almost all profit levels the company owners pay less tax than the partners. For example, when profits are £50,000 the tax saving is £2,536, when profits are £100,000 the tax saving is £7,594 and when profits are £250,000 the tax saving is £14,313.

On average, the company owners get to keep an extra 5% of the profits of the business, i.e. their overall tax rate is five percentage points lower. Remember this is the *annual saving* – it may be possible to enjoy similar savings every year.

However, when profits are quite modest, a company will not produce any tax savings at all or will only produce modest savings. For example, when profits are less than £20,000 the company owners end up paying more tax. When profits are £30,000 the total tax saving is just £736.

TABLE 6
Company vs Partnership 2014/15
Profits Taken as £7,956 Salary & Dividends

Profits £	Company Tax £	Partnership £	Saving £
20,000	818	654	-164
30,000	2,818	3,554	736
40,000	4,818	6,454	1,636
50,000	6,818	9,354	2,536
60,000	8,818	12,254	3,436
70,000	10,818	15,154	4,336
80,000	12,818	18,054	5,236
90,000	14,818	21,769	6,951
100,000	18,376	25,970	7,594
110,000	22,376	30,169	7,793
120,000	26,376	34,369	7,993
130,000	30,376	38,569	8,193
140,000	34,376	42,769	8,393
150,000	38,376	46,969	8,593
160,000	42,376	51,169	8,793
170,000	46,376	55,369	8,993
180,000	50,376	59,569	9,193
190,000	54,376	63,769	9,393
200,000	58,376	67,969	9,593
210,000	62,376	74,169	11,793
220,000	66,376	80,369	13,993
230,000	71,075	86,569	15,494
240,000	76,768	92,769	16,001
250,000	82,656	96,969	14,313
260,000	88,545	101,169	12,624
270,000	94,059	105,369	11,310
280,000	98,059	109,569	11,510
290,000	102,059	113,769	11,710
300,000	106,059	117,969	11,910

How the Tax Savings Are Calculated

Taking a sample profit figure from Table 6 – £100,000 – let's examine how the numbers are calculated:

Partnership Tax Calculation

Each partner pays tax on £50,000 of profits:

Income tax:	£
Profit share	50,000
Less: Personal allowance	10,000
Taxable profits	40,000
£31,865 @ 20%	6,373
£8,135 @ 40%	3,254
Total	9,627

National insurance:	
Class 2 (£2.75 x 52)	143
Class 4:	
£41,865 - £7,956 @ 9%	3,052
£50,000 - £41,865 @ 2%	163
Total	3,358

Income tax and national insurance per partner: £12,985
Combined income tax and national insurance: £25,970

Company Tax Calculation

Corporation tax:	£
Profits	100,000
Less: salaries (£7,956 x 2)	15,912
Taxable profits	84,088
Corporation tax @ 20%	16,818
After-tax profits	67,270

Income tax on dividend - each:	
Cash dividend (£67,270/2)	33,635
Gross dividend (£33,635/0.9)	37,372
Tax-free (£41,865 - £7,956)	33,909
Taxed @ 22.5% (£37,372 - £33,909)	3,463
Income tax - each	779

Total corporation tax and income tax: £18,376

Reinvesting Profits to Boost Tax Savings

As we know company owners can keep profits in the company or extract them as income. Only corporation tax is payable on profits kept in the company. The company owners do not have to pay any additional income tax. By contrast, self-employed business owners pay income tax and national insurance on ALL of their profits.

Table 7 compares the total tax payable by two company owners with the total tax payable by two business partners. The company owners take a salary of £7,956 each and the rest of their income as dividends. The difference between this table and Table 6 above is that the company owners only extract 50% of the after-tax profits. The remaining profits are kept inside the company.

Once again we see that, when profits are reinvested, a company can produce bigger tax savings. For example, when profits are £100,000 the total tax saving is £9,151 (£7,594 when all profits are extracted), when profits are £150,000 the total tax saving is £20,151 (£8,593 when all profits are extracted) and when profits are £240,000 the total tax saving is £40,801 (£16,001 when all profits are extracted).

On average, the company owners get to keep 12% more of the profits than the partnership! Remember this is the *annual saving* – it may be possible to enjoy similar savings every year.

When Reinvesting Does Not Save Tax

When profits are roughly £90,000 or less, reinvesting produces no additional tax savings. In other words, the tax savings in Table 7 are identical to the tax savings in Table 6. Don't get me wrong, you will still pay less tax than a partnership at most profit levels. But you cannot increase your tax savings further by reinvesting.

This is because reinvesting profits helps company owners save *income tax* but they only pay income tax on their dividends when they become higher-rate taxpayers (income over £41,865 *each*).

Thus a company with profits of roughly £90,000 and two owners can pay out all its after-tax profits as tax-free dividends (assuming of course that the directors have no other income).

TABLE 7
Total Tax Bills Compared
Two Owners - 50% Profit Reinvested

Profits £	Company £	Partnership £	Saving £
20,000	818	654	-164
30,000	2,818	3,554	736
40,000	4,818	6,454	1,636
50,000	6,818	9,354	2,536
60,000	8,818	12,254	3,436
70,000	10,818	15,154	4,336
80,000	12,818	18,054	5,236
90,000	14,818	21,769	6,951
100,000	16,818	25,969	9,151
110,000	18,818	30,169	11,351
120,000	20,818	34,369	13,551
130,000	22,818	38,569	15,751
140,000	24,818	42,769	17,951
150,000	26,818	46,969	20,151
160,000	28,818	51,169	22,351
170,000	30,968	55,369	24,401
180,000	33,968	59,569	25,601
190,000	36,968	63,769	26,801
200,000	39,968	67,969	28,001
210,000	42,968	74,169	31,201
220,000	45,968	80,369	34,401
230,000	48,968	86,569	37,601
240,000	51,968	92,769	40,801
250,000	54,968	96,969	42,001
260,000	57,968	101,169	43,201
270,000	60,968	105,369	44,401
280,000	63,968	109,569	45,601
290,000	66,968	113,769	46,801
300,000	69,968	117,969	48,001

How the Tax Savings Are Calculated

Taking a sample profit figure from Table 7 – £200,000 – let's examine how the company tax numbers are calculated (the partnership figures are the same as in Table 6):

Company Tax Calculation

Corporation tax:	£
Profits	200,000
Less: salaries (£7,956 x 2)	15,912
Taxable profits	184,088
Corporation tax @ 20%	36,818
After-tax profits	147,270

After-tax profits:	£
Reinvested (£147,270 x 50%)	73,635
Cash dividends	73,635
Cash dividends – each (£73,635/2)	36,818

Income tax - each	
Gross dividend (36,818/0.9)	40,908
Tax-free (£41,865 - £7,956)	33,909
Taxed @ 22.5% (£40,908 - £33,909)	6,999
Income tax	1,575

Income tax – combined	
£1,575 x 2	3,150

Total corporation tax and income tax: £39,968

A partnership with identical profits will pay £67,969 in tax.

One Shareholder versus Two Shareholders

So far we've compared the tax paid by company owners with the tax paid by sole traders and partnerships.

Another interesting question is:

How much tax is saved if a company has two owners instead of one?

Table 8 compares the total tax (corporation tax and income tax) payable by one company owner with the total tax payable by two company owners.

The figures come from Table 6 above and Table 4 in Chapter 13.

Clearly, involving your spouse/partner in the business could produce significant additional tax savings. For example, if profits are £50,000 your spouse could save you £2,370 in tax. If profits are £100,000 your spouse could save you £10,812 in tax!

The basic idea is that, by involving your spouse/partner, you can benefit from two tax-free salaries and two lots of tax-free dividends. By splitting your income it also takes longer to reach the £100,000 and £150,000 thresholds where extortionate tax rates kick in.

Looking at the table, when profits are £40,000 or less your spouse will save you £1,591 in tax. This is the corporation tax relief on the second salary. There is no additional tax saving because the company owner is below the higher-rate threshold, i.e. his dividends are tax free whether all the profits come to him or are split with his spouse.

Note that the tax savings will be smaller or disappear altogether if the spouse/partner has income from other sources, e.g. another job or business or portfolio of rental properties.

Furthermore, when it comes to paying salaries and dividends to your spouse there are certain traps you have to watch out for, as we shall now see.

TABLE 8
One versus Two Company Owners
Profits Taken as £7,956 Salary & Dividends

Profits £	One Owner £	Two Owners £	Saving £
20,000	2,409	818	1,591
30,000	4,409	2,818	1,591
40,000	6,409	4,818	1,591
50,000	9,188	6,818	2,370
60,000	13,188	8,818	4,370
70,000	17,188	10,818	6,370
80,000	21,188	12,818	8,370
90,000	25,188	14,818	10,370
100,000	29,188	18,376	10,812
110,000	33,188	22,376	10,812
120,000	38,384	26,376	12,008
130,000	44,273	30,376	13,897
140,000	49,029	34,376	14,653
150,000	53,029	38,376	14,653
160,000	57,029	42,376	14,653
170,000	61,129	46,376	14,753
180,000	65,573	50,376	15,197
190,000	70,018	54,376	15,642
200,000	74,462	58,376	16,086
210,000	78,907	62,376	16,531
220,000	83,351	66,376	16,975
230,000	87,796	71,075	16,721
240,000	92,240	76,768	15,473
250,000	96,685	82,656	14,028
260,000	101,129	88,545	12,584
270,000	105,573	94,059	11,515
280,000	110,018	98,059	11,959
290,000	114,462	102,059	12,404
300,000	118,907	106,059	12,848

Chapter 23

Splitting Income: Practical Issues

In Chapter 22 it was shown that a couple may be able to double up the tax-free salary and dividend.

That's all very well if the couple own and run the company together. But what if your spouse/partner isn't involved in the business, for example if the company was started before you met or if your spouse/partner has a separate career and receives salary income from another employer?

In situations like these it may be possible to save income tax by gifting shares in the company to your spouse. It may even be possible to save more tax by paying them a salary as well.

How much tax can be saved depends on individual circumstances, for example how much profit the company makes and how much taxable income each person has already.

Capital Gains Tax

If you wish to split your dividend income with your spouse you generally have to transfer shares in the company to them.

In the case of married couples, a transfer of shares would be exempt from capital gains tax.

In the case of unmarried couples it gets a bit more complicated. Any transfer of shares in the business would be treated as if a sale has taken place at market value. However, the couple can jointly elect to claim holdover relief. What this means is that the transfer is treated as having taken place at a price equal to the original purchase price of the shares. This means there will be no capital gains tax payable on the transfer.

To qualify for holdover relief, however, the company must generally be a regular trading company.

Unmarried couples who want to split their income face a further potential danger (see below).

Giving the Business Away

To successfully split your dividend income with your spouse it is essential that proper ownership of shares in the company is handed over. This means your spouse must be able to do what they like with any dividends paid out and with any capital growth from any sale of the business.

As we shall see shortly, it is also safer to transfer ordinary shares rather than shares that have fewer voting rights or other rights.

It is probably advisable to have any dividends received by your spouse paid into a separate bank account in their name, to illustrate to HMRC that you have not retained control of the money.

Dividends are generally payable in proportion to shareholdings. So if you normally take a dividend of £100,000 and want to transfer £40,000 of this income to your spouse, you will generally have to transfer 40% of the business to them.

Because this sort of tax planning, if done correctly, involves effectively giving away ownership and control of part of your business, it is only suitable where there is a significant amount of trust between the parties involved.

How Much of the Business Should Be Transferred?

For many company owners, a 50:50 ownership split with their spouse or partner will prove optimal, but a smaller stake can be transferred if the founder wants to retain more control over the business.

Spouse Has No Taxable Income

This is the 'bread and butter' scenario. The company owner is a higher-rate taxpayer; the spouse is a 'house-spouse' with no job and no other taxable income.

The spouse can receive gross dividends of up to £41,865 in 2014/15 (£37,679 cash dividends). The maximum potential tax saving is £9,420 if the other spouse is a higher-rate taxpayer (£37,679 x 25%).

If the company owner is an additional rate taxpayer (income over £150,000) the potential tax saving would be £11,530 (£37,679 x 30.6%).

Spouse is a Basic-Rate Taxpayer

Another potentially common scenario. The company owner is a higher-rate taxpayer; their spouse has some taxable income but is a basic-rate taxpayer (income under £41,865 in 2014/15). The spouse's taxable income could come from a job, a sole trader business, rental properties etc.

For example, let's say your spouse already has taxable income of £30,000 from other sources. They can receive tax-free gross dividends of up to £11,865 in 2014/15 (£10,679 in cash dividends). The potential tax saving is £2,670 (£10,679 x 25%).

If the company owner is an additional rate taxpayer the potential tax saving would be £3,268 (£10,679 x 30.6%).

Spouse is a Higher-Rate Taxpayer

In this situation both partners have taxable income of more than £41,865 (2014/15 figures). The spouse's income comes from other sources.

In this situation paying dividends to the spouse will only produce a tax saving if the company owner pays income tax at more than 25%.

For example, if the company owner is an additional rate taxpayer any dividends paid to their spouse will be taxed at 25% instead of 30.6%. Potential tax saving: £560 per £10,000 of cash dividends paid.

There are many reasons why any tax savings that may be achieved in one tax year by splitting income with your spouse may not be achievable in full in future tax years, including:

- Changes to tax rates and thresholds
- Changes to personal circumstances

Changes to Tax Rates & Thresholds

The additional rate applying to income over £150,000 was reduced on 6 April 2013. The effective tax rate applying to cash dividends was reduced from 36.1% to 30.6%. The potential tax saving that can be achieved by transferring dividend income to a spouse who is a higher-rate taxpayer has been reduced from £1,110 per £10,000 of cash dividends to £560.

Of course, where your spouse is a basic-rate taxpayer and can receive tax-free dividends the savings are still impressive: 30.6% tax versus 0% tax.

The Government has stated that it is committed to abolishing the additional rate altogether but this will be politically difficult and no firm date has been provided. If the rate were to be abolished this could eliminate the tax savings currently achieved from shifting dividend income to a spouse who is a higher-rate taxpayer

Changes to Personal Circumstances

The income tax savings obtained by splitting income with a spouse are only achieved if the current company owner has a higher marginal income tax rate than their spouse.

It is possible that, over time, the original company owner's marginal income tax rate will fall and/or the tax rate of his spouse will increase. This could eliminate or even reverse any initial income tax saving that is achieved.

The original company owner's marginal tax rate could fall if the company's profits fall, resulting in lower dividends. The marginal tax rate of a spouse could rise if their income from other sources increases (for example, if a sole trader business they own produces bigger profits).

There are lots of different permutations. The key point is that couples should look further ahead than just one tax year when deciding what proportion of the company each should own.

HMRC's Attacks on Income Shifting

Income splitting arrangements like those described in this chapter have come under attack in recent years. In particular, the taxman has tried to prevent dividends being paid to non-working spouses or spouses who do just a small amount of work for the company.

In particular, the taxman's target has been small 'personal service' companies (IT consultants and the like) where most of the work is carried out by one person.

It all came to a head in the notorious 'Arctic Systems' tax case. HMRC tried to use the so-called settlements legislation to prevent Geoff Jones, a computer consultant, from splitting his dividend income with his wife.

The settlements legislation is designed to prevent income being shifted from one individual to another via a 'settlement', for example by transferring an asset or making some other 'arrangement'.

In the Arctic Systems case Mr Jones did most of the work in the company. Mrs Jones did a few hours admin each week. Because Mr Jones only paid himself a small salary despite all the work he did, more money was left to pay out as dividends to Mrs Jones. HMRC therefore decided that a settlement had taken place and tried to have Mrs Jones' dividend income taxed in her husband's hands.

HMRC originally won the case but the decision was overturned by the House of Lords.

The judges agreed with HMRC that a settlement had taken place **but** decided that the settlement provisions could not be applied because in this case the couple were protected by the exemption for gifts between spouses. This exemption applies where:

- There is an outright gift of property to a spouse, and
- The property is not wholly or mainly a right to income

On the first point, the judges ruled that, although Mrs Jones had subscribed for her share when the company was set up (i.e., it was not strictly speaking gifted to her by her husband), her share was essentially a gift because it contained an 'element of bounty': the share provided a benefit that Mr Jones would not have given to a complete stranger.

On the second point, the judges also ruled that a gift of ordinary shares is not wholly or mainly a right to income because ordinary shares have other rights: voting rights and the right to capital gains if the company is sold.

Thanks to the courage of Mr and Mrs Jones, who were prepared to fight HMRC all the way to the House of Lords, this exemption should safeguard most types of income splitting arrangements between married couples where ordinary shares are involved.

For this reason many tax advisers are of the opinion that married couples should make hay while the sun shines, i.e. they should split their dividend income with their spouses while they can.

Preference Shares

The outcome of the Arctic Systems case may have been different if another type of share other than ordinary shares had been involved.

In another tax case (*Young v Pearce*), wives were issued with preference shares that paid income but had very few other rights. The shares did not have voting rights and did not entitle the spouses to receive any payout in the event of the company being sold (other than the original £25 payment for the shares).

All that the preference shares provided was a right to receive 30% of the company's profits as a dividend. The court therefore decided that the preference shares provided wholly or mainly a right to income. Thus the exemption for gifts between spouses was not available and the settlement rules applied. The wives' dividends were therefore taxed in the hands of their husbands.

Unmarried Couples & Other Family Members

Although HMRC was defeated in the Arctic Systems case, the judges did agree that a settlement had taken place. The taxpayers only won the case thanks to the exemption for gifts between spouses.

There is now uncertainty as to where this leaves income-splitting arrangements between other groups of individuals, in particular, unmarried couples.

HMRC probably does take the view that the settlements legislation applies to unmarried couples and other family members, especially where small personal service companies are involved.

However, to date the taxman has not pursued these individuals aggressively so, again, it may be a case of making hay while the sun shines.

To protect against any potential attack the best defence is probably to have both individuals equally involved in the business (a bit of admin or bookkeeping will not suffice, as Mr and Mrs Jones discovered.)

HMRC's main concern seems to be personal service companies (IT consultants and other businesses where the profits are generated from one person's services). Larger businesses that have other employees, premises, equipment etc may be safer because the profits come from various sources, not just the work of one individual.

Danger Ahead?

In 2007 draft income shifting legislation was published but fortunately never made it onto the statute books after being widely condemned for being completely unworkable.

That draft legislation essentially sought to prevent business owners from receiving dividends unless they effectively earned them! This goes against the whole basis of shareholder capitalism – dividends are supposed to be a reward for being an entrepreneur and setting up or investing in a business.

Although income shifting legislation is on the back burner for now, it could be introduced in the future and could upset some income splitting arrangements.

If legislation is introduced eventually it may be important to demonstrate that the shareholders are fully involved in the business.

Salaries for Spouses

If your partner also works for your company they can be paid a salary. Please note, you cannot pay them a salary if they do no work for the company. And you cannot pay them more than the market rate. If you do, the company will be denied tax relief for the expense.

If your partner has no taxable income from other sources, a small salary will be more tax efficient than simply paying them dividends.

Why? Unlike dividends which are paid out of the company's after-tax profits, salaries are a tax deductible expense for the company.

In other words, in addition to any income tax savings enjoyed by couples who split their income, a salary will also save the company corporation tax.

For example, a small salary of £7,956 will save a small company £1,591 in corporation tax.

To avoid national insurance, salary payments should be made monthly instead of as a lump sum. If, however, your spouse is a director the payment can be made as a lump sum because company directors pay national insurance on an annual basis.

Second Jobs

What if your spouse already has income from other sources, e.g. a salary from another job? Is it still tax efficient to get your company to pay them a salary?

Firstly, it's important to point out that, if your spouse works for another employer, the employment contract may prevent them working for you as well.

Even if there is no such restriction, it is usually not more tax efficient to receive a salary where there is income from other sources that uses up all of the individual's income tax personal allowance (although there may be other reasons why a salary is desirable).

Part 6

Controlling Your Tax Bill

Chapter 24

Company Owners Can Control Their Income Tax Bills

A company owner can often decide whether any distribution of the company's money is classified as salary or dividend.

Another advantage of being a company owner is that you have complete control over *how much* income you withdraw in total.

This gives you significant control over your personal income tax bill.

Unlike sole traders, who pay tax each year on ALL the profits of the business, company owners only pay income tax on the money they actually withdraw from the company.

This allows company owners to reduce their income tax bills by adopting the following strategies:

- 'Smooth income'
- 'Roller-coaster income'

Smooth Income

With smooth income, the company owner withdraws roughly the same amount of money each year, even though the company's profits may fluctuate considerably.

'Smooth income' allows the director/shareholder to stay below any of the following key income tax thresholds that could result in a higher income tax bill:

- £41,865   Higher-rate tax
- £50,000   Child benefit tax charge (see Chapter 25)
- £100,000   Personal allowance withdrawal
- £150,000   Additional rate tax

The last three thresholds didn't even exist a few years ago, which goes to show how much more complicated and burdensome the UK's income tax system has become for those considered to be 'high earners'.

Roller-coaster Income

With 'roller-coaster income', the company owners take a bigger or smaller salary or dividend than would normally be required to fund their lifestyles.

Roller-coaster income could save you tax in the following circumstances:

Tax Rates Are Going Up Or Down

If the Government announces that tax rates will rise during a future tax year, you may wish to pay yourself more income now and less income later on.

And if your tax rate will fall during a future tax year, you should pay yourself less income now and more income later on.

Two recent tax changes that we were all warned about well in advance include the child benefit charge and the reduction in the additional rate of tax from 50% to 45%.

You Want to Avoid Capital Gains Tax

It may also make sense for company owners to pay themselves less income during tax years in which they sell assets subject to capital gains tax, e.g. rental properties.

Why? This may allow some of your basic-rate band (£31,865 in 2014/15) to be freed up, which means some of your capital gains will be taxed at 18% instead of 28% (see Chapter 27).

Pension Income

When you reach age 55 you may decide to start withdrawing money from any private pension scheme you belong to, for example a self-invested personal pension (SIPP). Any amount you withdraw over and above your 25% tax-free lump sum will be subject to income tax.

Fortunately, if you opt for a pension drawdown arrangement, you can vary the amount of income you withdraw from your pension scheme every year (from April 2015 there will be no limits placed on the amount of income you can withdraw).

Coupled with the fact that you can vary the amount of income you withdraw from your company, this could allow you to minimise your income tax bill by staying below any of the income tax thresholds listed earlier.

Chapter 25

Using a Company to Protect Your Child Benefit

Child benefit is gradually withdrawn where any member of a household has over £50,000 income. This is done by imposing a High Income Child Benefit Charge on the highest earner in the household.

Once the highest earner's income reaches £60,000, all of the child benefit will effectively have been taken away in higher tax charges.

The £50,000 threshold can be increased or decreased by the Government but will not automatically increase with inflation. In other words, over time more and more taxpayers may face paying the new child benefit tax charge.

Company owners can avoid the child benefit charge by altering the amount of income they extract from their companies. In other words, they can keep their incomes below £50,000 in some or all tax years. Self-employed business owners cannot do this.

Child Benefit: How Much is it Worth?

Child benefit is an extremely valuable *tax-free* handout from the Government. Parents who qualify currently receive:

- £1,066 for the first child
- £704.60 for each subsequent child

Depending on the number of children, a family can expect to receive the following total child benefit payment in 2014/15:

Children	Total Child Benefit
1	£1,066
2	£1,771
3	£2,475
4	£3,180

plus £704.60 for each additional child

How Long Do Child Benefit Payments Continue?

Child benefit generally continues to be paid until your children are 16 years old.

The payments will continue until age 20 if the child is enrolled in full-time 'non-advanced' education, including:

- GCSEs
- A levels
- Scottish Highers
- NVQ/SVQ level 1, 2 or 3
- BTEC National Diploma, National Certificate, 1st Diploma

So if your child is 16, 17, 18 or 19 and enrolled in one of the above courses, child benefit will continue to be paid.

Once the child is 20 years old all child benefit payments will cease.

The following courses do NOT qualify:

- Degrees
- Diploma of Higher Education
- NVQ level 4 or above
- HNCs or HNDs
- Teacher training

In other words, if your children are 16, 17, 18 or 19 and enrolled in any these courses, you will not receive any child benefit.

Total Value of Child Benefit

Child benefit payments continue for between 16 and 20 years. Based on current child benefit rates, the total amount you can expect to receive over the total period your child qualifies is:

- £17,056 to £21,320 tax free for the first child
- £11,274 to £14,092 tax free for each additional child

These are very much 'back of the envelope' figures because they ignore the potential danger that child benefit may not be increased in line with inflation in the years ahead.

However, they clearly illustrate how valuable child benefit is over many years and why it is worth protecting where possible.

The £50,000 Threshold for Company Owners

As in previous chapters, we have to distinguish between gross dividends and cash dividends. To avoid the child benefit charge you have to keep your salary and *gross* dividends below £50,000.

In previous chapters we have shown that company owners can take a total tax-free income comprising salary and gross dividends of £41,865. This leaves you scope to pay an additional gross dividend of £8,135 before the child benefit charge comes into force.

In cash terms, a company owner who wants to avoid the child benefit charge in 2014/15 could take a tax-free salary of £7,956 plus tax-free cash dividends of £30,518 plus additional taxable cash dividends of £7,321. The total income tax payable on the additional dividend will be £1,830 (£7,321 x 25%). Total *after-tax* income: £43,965.

For a company owned and managed by a couple, the above amounts can be doubled up. Total after-tax income: £87,930.

Income between £50,000 and £60,000

If you want to extract more income from your company you will face paying the High Income Child Benefit Charge.

For every £100 of income over £50,000 a tax charge equivalent to 1% of the child benefit is levied on the highest earner in the household.

For example, if the highest earner in the household has income of £55,000, the tax charge will be equivalent to 50% of the child benefit claimed.

If the highest earner in the household has income of £60,000 or more, the tax charge will be 100% of the child benefit claimed.

For the highest earner in the household the child benefit charge creates the following marginal tax rates on dividend income in the £50,000-£60,000 tax bracket:

Children	Marginal Tax Rate on Cash Dividends
1	37%
2	45%
3	53%
4	60%

Plus 8% for each additional child.

Example

David, a company owner, has taken a salary and gross dividends totalling £50,000 so far in 2014/15. He is the highest earner in a household claiming child benefit for two children.

David decides to withdraw an additional gross dividend of £10,000. His total income will be £60,000 so he will face the maximum child benefit charge. The tax payable on the additional dividend is £4,021, calculated as follows:

£9,000 cash dividend x 25%	*£2,250*
£1,771 child benefit x 100%	*£1,771*
Total additional tax	*£4,021*

The effective tax rate on the additional £9,000 cash dividend is 45%.

Income between £60,000 and £100,000

If your income is at least £60,000 you will already be paying the maximum child benefit charge. Income between £60,000 and £100,000 does not incur any further child benefit charge.

Gross dividends between £60,000 and £100,000 will continue to be taxed at an effective income tax rate of 25% of the cash amount.

Once your income rises above £100,000 you face a fresh tax sting: withdrawal of the income tax personal allowance.

How to Avoid the Child Benefit Charge

Clearly taxpayers have an enormous incentive to escape the much higher tax rates that apply to dividends in the £50,000-£60,000 bracket. Company owners may find it easier than other taxpayers to escape the child benefit charge because they can alter the amount of dividend income they receive each year. Some company owners may be able to avoid the new charge altogether by keeping their income below £50,000.

Others, including those who usually withdraw more than £60,000 each year, may be able to avoid the charge in some tax years but not others, or partly reduce the charge.

Company owners can also spread their income among family members, for example by gifting shares in the business to their spouse (see Chapter 23).

For the current and future tax years, the following dividend strategies could be considered (figures quoted include gross dividends in each case):

Smooth Income

If the income you withdraw is currently somewhere between the higher-rate threshold and £50,000 and you expect your income to continue growing, you could consider extracting approximately £50,000 for several tax years, where possible.

This may mean you pay yourself more income than you need to begin with and less income than you need later on but you may be able to avoid the child benefit charge completely for several years.

Roller-Coaster Income

If you plan to withdraw over £60,000 from 2014/15 onwards, you could consider taking big dividends during some tax years and smaller ones in other tax years.

For example, instead of taking income of £75,000 every year, consider taking £100,000 every second year, if possible, and £50,000 in the intervening years. This will allow you to avoid the child benefit charge every second year.

Similarly, a company owner who normally takes £60,000 every year could consider taking £70,000 in year 1 and £50,000 in year 2, where possible.

Austerity

If your taxable income is normally over £50,000, you could consider keeping your income below £50,000 for several years to avoid the child benefit charge.

For example, let's say you have three children and your taxable income is normally £60,000. If for the next three years you can afford to withdraw just £50,000, you may be able to protect over £7,000 of child benefit.

Other Issues

When paying yourself dividends that are smaller than normal or bigger than normal there may be lots of other issues to consider. For example, you can only declare bigger dividends if the company has sufficient distributable profits.

If you postpone taking some of your dividends until a future tax year you may leave yourself exposed to any future increase in tax on company owners. Remember, tax rules are constantly changing.

Chapter 26

Business Owners with Income from Other Sources

Introduction

In Chapter 24 we explained why company owners, in deciding how much income to withdraw from their companies, need to be aware of the following income tax thresholds and brackets:

- Over £41,865   Higher rate tax
- £50,000-£60,000   Child benefit tax charge
- £100,000-£120,000   Personal allowance withdrawal
- Over £150,000   Additional rate of tax

The general rule is that a combined income of less than £41,865 (made up of a small salary and dividends) is tax free. Additional cash dividends are generally taxed at 25%. However, income that falls into the final three tax brackets is taxed at much higher rates:

- £50,000-£60,000   37% to 60% or more
- £100,000-£120,000   37.5% to 46%
- Over £150,000   30.6%

(Note: these are the tax rates applying to cash dividends although the thresholds apply to gross dividends. The £50,000-£60,000 threshold only applies to households in receipt of child benefit.)

When trying to avoid these extortionate tax rates, you must remember to include any other taxable income you receive. Income from other sources could force your company income, in particular your dividend income, into a higher tax bracket.

To avoid a potential tax sting you may wish to reduce the amount of income you withdraw from your company. Company owners can vary their income from year to year but the self-employed (sole traders and partnerships) have far less flexibility. Being able to control your taxable income is one of the major benefits of using a company.

The Order in which Income is Taxed

Income is taxed in the following order:

- Non-savings income:
  - ➤ Employment income
  - ➤ Self-employment income
  - ➤ Rental income
- Savings income
- Dividend income

Dividends are always treated as the top slice of income.

Let's say you expect to earn £10,000 of rental income during the current tax year but, so far, have not withdrawn any income from your company. As things stand, all of your rental income will be tax free, being covered by your income tax personal allowance.

Let's say you now decide to withdraw a tax-free salary of £7,956 and a tax-free cash dividend of £30,518 from your company.

The decision to take a salary means you now have £17,956 of non-savings income and your income tax bill will increase by £1,591:

£17,956 - £10,000 personal allowance = £7,956 x 20% = £1,591

Effectively, you've paid 20% tax on your salary.

And what about your supposedly 'tax-free' dividends?

Your non-savings income uses up £7,956 of your basic-rate band, which means £7,956 of your gross dividends (£7,160 of your cash dividends) will now be pushed into the higher-rate tax bracket.

As a result, your dividends will no longer be completely tax free. There will be an income tax bill of £1,790 (£7,160 x 25%).

Income from Other Sources

With the exception of self-employment income, it may be possible to extract all of the various types of income listed above from your own company: employment income, rental income, interest income, and dividend income.

We've already talked extensively about salaries (employment income) and dividends. If your company uses a property that you own personally (for example, an office or shop) it can also pay you rent; and if your company borrows money from you it can pay you interest.

In this chapter the focus is on company owners who have income from *other sources* – i.e. income that does not come out of their own company.

More specifically, the focus is on company owners who have income from other sources that is subject to *income tax*.

Some income (e.g. most interest income and stock market dividends) can be sheltered from income tax inside an ISA or pension scheme.

It is even possible to shelter assets from income tax inside a company. Some property investors do this. Corporation tax will still be payable on any rental profits produced by the properties but the income tax position of the company owner will be unaffected, unless those profits are extracted.

Most company owners have at least some taxable income from other sources but the amounts are often trivial and can, by and large, be ignored (e.g. a few pounds of bank interest).

Those company owners who do have a significant amount of taxable income from other sources, and cannot shelter it from income tax, may wish to reduce the amount of income they withdraw from their own companies so as to avoid paying income tax at some of the extortionate rates listed at the beginning of this chapter.

Other Income – Control

One of the benefits of being a company owner is that you can to a great extent control how much income you withdraw from your business. This allows you to control your income tax bill from year to year.

Income from other sources is often less easy to control. For example, it may not be possible to shift it from one tax year into another tax year. You may be able to control the dividends declared by your own company but you cannot force the board of Vodafone to increase or lower its dividend!

Company owners who want to keep their taxable income just below any of the key income tax thresholds may therefore have to increase or decrease their *company income* – it may not always be possible to alter income from other sources.

Gross Dividends vs Cash Dividends

If you have income from other sources and want to ensure that your dividend income does not breach the £41,865, £50,000, £100,000, or £150,000 thresholds, it is critical to remember that it is your gross dividends that are relevant, not the cash dividends you receive from your company.

Example

Maria owns a small company and decides to pay herself a salary of £7,956. She also has rental profits of £10,000 from some buy-to-let properties. She wants to take a big dividend out of her company but does not want her taxable income to exceed £100,000, the point at which her personal allowance will be withdrawn.

How much dividend income can she withdraw? She already has income of £17,956, which means she can withdraw a gross dividend of £82,044 (£100,000 - £17,956). The maximum cash dividend she can withdraw is £73,840 (£82,044 x 0.9).

Table 9 shows the maximum cash dividend you can withdraw during 2014/15 if you have other taxable income (including employment income) and want to avoid some of the key income tax thresholds.

TABLE 9
Avoiding the Tax Thresholds
Maximum Cash Dividend 2014/15

Other Income	Threshold £41,865	£50,000	£100,000
£7,956	£30,518	£37,840	£82,840
£10,000	£28,679	£36,000	£81,000
£15,000	£24,179	£31,500	£76,500
£20,000	£19,679	£27,000	£72,000
£25,000	£15,179	£22,500	£67,500
£30,000	£10,679	£18,000	£63,000
£35,000	£6,179	£13,500	£58,500
£40,000	£1,679	£9,000	£54,000
£45,000	£0	£4,500	£49,500
£50,000	£0	£0	£45,000

Note: Table may contain small rounding errors

For example, if you have other taxable income of £20,000 a cash dividend of £19,679 will keep your income below £41,865 and be completely tax free.

A cash dividend of up to £27,000 will ensure that your income does not exceed £50,000. Some of the dividend income will be taxable but you will avoid the child benefit tax charge.

A cash dividend of up to £72,000 will ensure that your income does not exceed £100,000. A significant amount of your dividend income will be taxed at 25% and you may end up paying the maximum child benefit tax charge but you will not lose any of your personal allowance.

Other Income –Predictability

At the start of a new tax year you may not know with complete certainty how much taxable income you will receive from other sources during the year. This could be problematic if you wish to withdraw dividends from your company *at the beginning of the tax year*.

If you withdraw dividends from your company and your other income then turns out to be higher than expected, you may end up paying more income tax than you expected on your company dividends.

Some types of income are, however, more predictable than others. For example, interest income, stock market dividends and rental income are arguably more predictable than, say, the profits of a sole trader business (self-employment income).

Some types of income, if not completely predictable, are more likely to end up being *less than expected*, rather than higher than expected. For example, a rental property that normally generates rental income of £1,000 per month may lie empty for three months, thereby producing an annual income of £9,000 rather than £12,000.

If your income from other sources turns out to be less than expected you may be able to get your company to pay you additional dividend income before the end of the tax year.

If your income from other sources turns out to be *higher than expected* you generally cannot reverse any dividends you have already taken out of your company, although it may be possible to do some emergency year-end tax planning, for example by making pension contributions.

Company owners who have unpredictable income from other sources may therefore wish to postpone paying dividends until closer to the end of the tax year if they are concerned that their dividend income may fall into a heavily taxed bracket.

Chapter 27

How to Pay 18% CGT by Postponing Dividends

Under the current capital gains tax rules there are three tax rates:

- 10% where Entrepreneurs Relief applies
- 18% for other gains made by basic-rate taxpayers
- 28% for other gains made by higher-rate taxpayers

Entrepreneurs Relief allows you to pay 10% tax when you sell your business. In all other cases, the amount of capital gains tax you pay depends on how much income you have earned during the tax year.

The maximum amount of capital gains that you can have taxed at 18% during the current tax year is £31,865. This is the amount of the basic-rate tax band for 2014/15.

Basic-rate taxpayers pay 10% less capital gains tax than higher-rate taxpayers. This means the basic-rate tax band can save each person up to £3,187 in capital gains tax this year:

£31,865 x 10% = £3,187

This creates some interesting tax-planning opportunities:

Income Planning

If you expect to realize a large capital gain, for example by disposing of a buy-to-let property, you may be able to save quite a lot of tax by making sure the disposal takes place during a tax year in which your taxable income is quite low.

In this respect, company owners can manipulate their incomes more easily than self-employed business owners. The company itself can keep trading and generating profits but the company owner can make sure that very little profit is extracted and taxed in his or her hands.

Example

Richard, a company owner, sells a buy-to-let property, realising a gain of £50,000 after deducting all buying and selling costs. Deducting his annual CGT exemption of £11,000 leaves a taxable gain of £39,000.

Richard hasn't paid himself any dividends during the current tax year and decides to postpone paying any so that £31,865 of his capital gain is taxed at 18%. The remaining £7,135 will be taxed at 28%. This simple piece of tax planning saves Richard £3,187 in capital gains tax.

Note that Richard can still pay himself a tax-free salary of up to £10,000 to utilise his income tax personal allowance. The income tax personal allowance does not interfere with the capital gains tax calculation. (In practice he may be better off paying himself a slightly smaller salary of £7,956 if his company doesn't have any spare employment allowance.)

Other income earners may find it more difficult to control their earnings in this manner.

Limitations

Although postponing dividends could help you pay less capital gains tax, it's probably not worth doing this unless you can withdraw the postponed dividends tax free in a future tax year.

If you take a bigger dividend in a later tax year, and end up paying 25% income tax, you may end up worse off overall.

Example continued

In the above example Richard postponed taking a gross dividend of £31,865 to free up his basic-rate band and pay 18% capital gains tax.

If during 2015/16 he takes an additional dividend of £31,865, on top off his usual salary and tax-free dividends, he will pay income tax of £7,170 (£31,865 x 22.5%). He saved £3,187 in capital gains tax in 2014/15 but pays an additional £7,170 of income tax in 2015/16. Overall Richard is £3,983 worse off.

Part 7

Using a Company: More Tax Benefits & Drawbacks

Chapter 28

Pension Contributions

If you want to make pension contributions there are three limits you need to know about:

- **The universal limit**. Everyone under 75 can make a pension contribution of £3,600 per year.

- **The earnings limit**. If you want to make bigger pension contributions, you must have *earnings*. For example, if your earnings are £30,000 the maximum pension contribution you can make is £30,000.

- **The annual allowance**. There is also an overall annual limit of £40,000 for contributions made by you and your employer (if you have one). So if your earnings are £60,000, the maximum contribution you (and your employer) can make is £40,000. You can also use any unused allowance from the previous three years. The annual allowance was reduced from £50,000 to £40,000 in April 2014.

Sole Traders

If you're self-employed your earnings are the pre-tax profits of the business (or your share if the business is a partnership).

For example, a sole trader with pre-tax profits (earnings) of £30,000 can make a pension contribution of £30,000. A sole trader with pre-tax profits of £80,000 can make a pension contribution of £40,000 (restricted by the annual allowance) but possibly £80,000 if he has enough unused allowance from the previous three years.

Company Owners

If you're a company owner your salary counts as earnings but your dividends do not. Dividends are investment income, so you cannot base your pension contributions on them.

A small company owner, taking a tax-free salary of, say, £7,956 during the current tax year, can therefore make a maximum pension contribution of £7,956. This is the *gross* contribution. The company owner would personally invest £6,365 and the taxman would top this up with £1,591 of basic-rate tax relief, producing a total pension contribution of £7,956.

Company owners with dividend income can enjoy 42.5% tax relief on their own pension contributions. Most higher-rate taxpayers only enjoy 40% tax relief on their pension contributions (see the Taxcafe guide *Pension Magic* for further details).

If a company owner wants to make a bigger pension contribution he can, of course, take a bigger salary. However, this is likely to have very unfavourable national insurance consequences. The national insurance on the additional salary could come to 25.8% (12% paid by the company owner, 13.8% paid by the company).

Company Pension Contributions

However, all is not lost. The company owner can get the *company* to make pension contributions on his behalf. Company pension contributions cannot exceed the annual allowance but can exceed your earnings.

Company pension contributions are very tax efficient. The contributions are a tax-deductible expense for the business (i.e. they attract corporation tax relief) and there are no income tax or national insurance consequences for the director or the company.

However, in some cases, there can be a risk that HMRC will deny corporation tax relief if the pension contribution, together with the company owner's other remuneration, amounts to more than a commercial rate of pay for the job they do for the company.

This problem is fairly rare but could affect any company owner who does not play a fully active role in the day to day management of their business.

Should Sole Traders Make Big Contributions?

Although sole traders and partners can make bigger pension contributions than many company owners (ignoring any contributions made by the company), that does not mean they should.

If you want to maximise your tax relief, you may wish to restrict the amount you invest. For example, if you have profits of £50,000 you may wish to make a gross pension contribution no higher than £8,135 (£50,000 - £41,865 higher-rate threshold). Why? This is the maximum contribution you can make if you want to enjoy higher-rate tax relief (i.e. 40% tax relief) on the entire contribution.

Summary

- Self-employed business owners (sole traders and partners) often have higher earnings than company owners and can therefore make bigger pension contributions.

- Company owners can get their companies to contribute to their pensions. Company contributions qualify for corporation tax relief and there are no income tax and national insurance consequences.

- However, corporation tax relief on company pension contributions can be denied in certain circumstances so there is arguably less certainty.

Chapter 29

Offset Mortgages

One of the benefits of being a sole trader or partnership, rather than running your business through a company, is you can earn much more interest on your cash. Interest rates on company savings accounts have been decimated in recent years and rates of 0.1% are not uncommon.

Sole traders and partners, because they are simply private individuals, can use any savings account and higher interest rates are readily available (although many of the better deals have restrictions or the special interest rate is whipped away after the first year).

Unlike companies, sole traders and partners can shelter money in a tax-free ISA each year. However, the problem here is that you cannot replace money taken out. So ISAs are no use to businesses which churn their cash or have large balances.

The problem with other savings accounts, however, is that 20%, 40%, or even more, of your interest goes to the taxman.

Tax-Free Interest

One way sole traders and partners can significantly boost the after-tax return on their cash is by switching their personal homes to offset mortgages.

The way it works is the bank stops paying you interest on your savings and starts charging you less interest on your mortgage.

That's fine, because not paying interest is always much better than earning it – not paying 4% interest is a lot better than earning, say, 1% after tax!

Example

Jean is a sole trader with £30,000 in her business bank account earning 1.5% per year. After paying 40% tax she is left with £270. With an offset mortgage her £30,000 business cash would be subtracted from her mortgage balance. If the mortgage interest rate is 4%, this will save her £1,200 interest per year: £30,000 x 4%. In summary, without an offset mortgage, Jean earns £270 interest net of tax; with an offset mortgage, she saves £1,200 per year – her overall saving is £930 per year.

You can calculate how much YOU could save as follows:

1. Find your mortgage interest rate – say 4%
2. Calculate the after-tax interest rate you earn on your business cash – say 0.9%
3. Subtract (2) from (1) – 3.1% in this example
4. Multiply the result in (3) by the average cash balance in your business

A business owner with £10,000 of cash will be £310 better off. With £200,000 cash, you could be £6,200 better off.

Other People's Money

Those who stand to benefit most from offset mortgages are, of course, those with lots of cash. However, the cash doesn't have to be your own – business owners can sometimes offset money that belongs to other people!

Why? Because the cash in your business account will include, not just your profits, but also things like VAT payable at the end of the quarter, income tax payments on account, employee's PAYE and national insurance, and amounts you owe creditors.

Eventually you will have to pay this money to someone but in the meantime it will save you from paying mortgage interest.

Further savings can be achieved by paying business expenses using a credit card. These expenses can be paid off interest free up to six weeks later, leaving more money in your bank account to offset your mortgage.

Drawbacks

Offset mortgage interest rates are rarely the lowest on offer but have become more competitive in recent years. If you have a significant amount of cash to offset you could still be much better off.

You will probably also have to pay one of those sneaky mortgage arrangement fees which could be £500 or more.

Finally, you may need to move banks. To maximise the benefit of an offset mortgage, you should be offsetting your business and personal savings accounts and your current accounts. This may require you to change bank if your existing one does not offer offset mortgages.

Company Owners

Company owners cannot offset the cash in their *company* bank accounts against their personal mortgages. So this is one of the tax benefits of being a sole trader (especially if your business holds lots of cash).

However, company owners can still benefit from offset mortgages. For example, if you pay yourself a big dividend at the start of every tax year, you could simply park the money in an offset mortgage bank account. This could save you a small fortune in mortgage interest over time – a relatively low-risk way to invest your dividends before spending them!

Chapter 30

Directors' Expenses

Company owners may find it more difficult than self-employed business owners to claim tax relief on certain expenses they incur personally, for example travel, subsistence and accommodation. These expenses will often be incurred by the director *personally* and then reimbursed by the company.

In most cases the company itself will get corporation tax relief if it reimburses the director's expenses (apart from expenses that are specifically disallowed, such as entertaining).

The director's own tax position is more complicated. Reimbursed expenses have to be included on the director's P11D. This is the form used to report expenses that are paid by the company and other benefits.

Although the director must include these reimbursements as a benefit-in-kind on his tax return, he may be able to claim a tax deduction for the expenses as well. This means there is no tax charge (although there is a lot of extra paperwork).

However, for the director's expenses to be tax deductible the test is more onerous than for self-employed business owners. Self-employed business owners can claim expenses that are incurred wholly and exclusively for the purposes of the business.

Company directors, on the other hand, are technically employees and can only claim expenses that are 'wholly, exclusively and **necessarily**' incurred for the purposes of their **employment**.

The key difference is that the company owner's expenses must be necessary and for their employment, rather than the business. As you can imagine, deciding whether an expense is 'necessary' or not is extremely subjective!

If the reimbursed expenses do not pass the 'wholly, exclusively and necessarily test' the director cannot claim a tax deduction and will have to pay income tax on the amount. The company will also have to pay employer's national insurance at 13.8%!

Travel Costs

Company directors can only claim travel costs that are incurred 'wholly, exclusively and necessarily' in the performance of their duties.

Sole traders only need to show that their trips are made for business purposes. Company owners need to show that they are necessary for their work.

Travelling first class shouldn't be a problem, however. You only have to show that the journey is necessary, not the method or class of travel.

Problems may arise when business trips are combined with holidays and if your spouse accompanies you on a business trip.

For example, let's say that in order to secure a large contract in a foreign country it is essential that you take your wife because it is the cultural norm in that country to be accompanied by your spouse. In this situation, the travel costs for the director's wife are arguably 'wholly, exclusively and necessarily' incurred and therefore tax deductible.

However, if it is merely desirable that your wife accompanies you, her travel costs will be a personal expense. The company could still get relief for those costs but the director would then be personally liable for a benefit in kind charge on them, giving rise to income tax and employer's national insurance.

The position is a little better for sole traders and business partners. Where their spouse accompanies them on a business trip, the spouse's presence on the trip only needs to be 'wholly and exclusively for business purposes' in order for the costs to be allowable. In other words her presence has to be desirable rather than essential.

However, even self-employed business owners face restrictions where there is a mixture of business and holiday, as is often the case with overseas travel.

Home Office Expenses

Sole traders and other self-employed individuals can claim a generous tax deduction if they use their own homes for business purposes.

They can claim a proportion of many household costs, including mortgage interest, council tax, heat and light, insurance and repairs.

This tax deduction is allowed even if the sole trader has other business premises but sometimes works from home because it is convenient.

For company directors it's not so simple. They have to show that it is necessary to work from home to carry out their employment duties. If they have other business premises and only work from home because it is convenient, HMRC will argue that it is not necessary to work from home.

One way a company director may be able to get around this restriction is by granting the company a non-exclusive licence to occupy a room in his home and charging the company rent. The rent must not exceed the market rate.

The rent will be taxable income but the director can claim the relevant proportion of the household running costs, potentially leaving him with a rental profit of zero and no tax to pay.

Meanwhile the company can claim a tax deduction for the rent paid to the director.

There are a couple of potential dangers if the agreement is not structured correctly. Firstly, there could be a partial restriction in the director's capital gains tax exemption on his home if any part of the home is used exclusively for business. There may also be business rates implications, although currently small business rate relief applies.

The director may need to ask their mortgage provider and home insurance provider for permission.

Dispensations

A dispensation is a notice from HMRC that removes the requirement to report certain expenses and benefits at the end of the tax year on the P11D. There is also no need to pay any tax or national insurance contributions on items covered by a dispensation.

The director cannot obtain tax relief if he has already been reimbursed by the company and the expense is covered by a dispensation.

The main expenses routinely covered by a dispensation are:

- Travel, including subsistence costs associated with business travel
- Fuel for company cars
- Hire car costs
- Telephones
- Business entertainment expenses
- Credit cards used for business
- Fees and subscriptions

Chapter 31

Losses

Self-Employed Business Owners

Where a self-employed person's business produces a loss, the general rule is that the loss is carried forward and offset against future profits from the business.

However, losses can also be set off against your **other income** (e.g. from a job or investments) or capital gains from the same tax year or the previous tax year.

This relief is even more generous if you have recently started your business. Losses that arise in the first four tax years of the business can be carried back and offset against your other income from the previous three tax years (earliest year first).

In other words, if you start a business and it makes a loss you can claim back tax you've paid in previous years.

The ability to offset losses against other income is extremely valuable. However, the amount you can claim is not unlimited. There is an annual cap on the total amount that can be claimed under this and various other tax reliefs.

The total amount of relief you can claim under all the affected reliefs in any one tax year is now limited to the greater of:

- £50,000, or
- 25% of your 'adjusted net income'

Broadly speaking, your adjusted net income is your total taxable income, after deducting gross pension contributions.

The cap does not apply, however, where a loss is set off against earlier profits *from the same trade*.

There are further restrictions for part-time business owners (those spending fewer than 10 hours per week working in the business). The maximum loss relief they can claim is restricted to £25,000.

In summary, if you're self-employed and make a loss you can offset the loss against your other income or capital gains from the same tax year or the previous tax year. Losses that arise in the first four tax years of the business can be carried back and offset against your other income from the previous three tax years.

These reliefs could produce welcome tax repayments. However, there is a limit (£50,000 per year in practice for most individuals) to the total amount of income tax relief that can be claimed.

Company Owners

Company owners have less flexibility than self-employed business owners. If your company makes a loss it cannot be offset against your *personal* income. The loss stays inside the company.

Trading losses can be offset against the company's other income (e.g. investment income) and capital gains from the same accounting period. Alternatively, the company can carry the loss forward and set it off against future profits from the same trade.

Companies can also make a claim to carry back losses and offset them against their profits and capital gains from the previous 12 months (where applicable). Carrying the loss back is an attractive option because it will generate a corporation tax repayment.

The company can only do this if it has already made a claim to first offset the loss against other income and capital gains from the same year.

There is no limit to the amount of trading loss relief available to companies. By contrast, individuals with trading losses are subject to the new £50,000 cap discussed above.

Summary

If you are starting a business and expect it to make losses initially, the way those losses are treated may influence your decision to set up a company or operate as a sole trader. If you have income from other sources (e.g. a job or investments) your trading losses could result in a tax repayment if you are self employed and this could provide a welcome cash boost at a difficult time.

Chapter 32

Cash Accounting

Sole traders and partnerships with small trading businesses may elect to be taxed under a new 'cash basis'. Companies and limited liability partnerships (LLPs) are among those who cannot use the cash basis.

The cash basis is generally only available if the annual turnover of the business does not exceed the VAT registration threshold (currently £81,000). However, once you are using the cash basis you can continue to use it, provided your turnover does not exceed twice the VAT registration threshold (currently £162,000).

Under the cash basis, income will be taxable only when it is received and expenditure will be deductible when it is paid. By contrast, under normal accounting principles (known as the accruals basis), income is taxed when it is *earned* and expenses are deductible when they are *incurred*.

The cash basis could be attractive to businesses that have to wait a long time to get paid by their suppliers.

Where the cash basis is used, there is no distinction between 'revenue' and 'capital' expenditure. Generally speaking revenue expenditure includes most of the day to day expenses of a business (e.g. salaries and stationery). Capital expenditure includes purchases of assets that normally qualify for capital allowances.

Under the cash basis capital expenditure can be claimed when it is paid but there are some restrictions:

- Cash basis deductions will only be available for capital expenditure if the item would otherwise qualify for plant and machinery capital allowances.

- The cost of vans or motor cycles can be claimed on a cash basis but the mileage allowances will then not be available (see Chapter 33).

- Motoring expenses for cars can be calculated using either existing capital allowances rules and actual expenditure or the simplified expenses mileage rates.

In addition to these restrictions, businesses using the cash basis will be limited to a maximum claim of £500 per year in respect of interest on cash borrowings.

Sideways loss relief will not be available, so you will not be able to offset losses against your other income (see Chapter 31). Losses arising under the cash basis can only be carried forward for set off against future profits from the same trade.

Chapter 33

Motoring Costs

Capital Allowances

Cars owned by self-employed business owners and companies enjoy the same capital allowance rates. For cars purchased from April 2013 onwards the allowances are as follows:

- CO_2 emissions over 130g/km   8% per year
- CO_2 emissions over 95g/km   18% per year
- CO_2 emissions 95g/km or less   100%

The 100% enhanced capital allowance for cars with low CO_2 emissions has been extended for a further three years to 31 March 2018. However, from April 2015 the CO_2 threshold will be reduced from 95g/km to 75g/km.

For cars owned by sole traders and partnerships the capital allowance claim is reduced to reflect private use of the vehicle. For example, a car purchased during 2014/15 for £10,000 which has 140g/km of CO_2 emissions and 50% private use will be eligible for an allowance of £400 (8% x £10,000 = £800, less 50%).

For cars owned by companies, there is no restriction in the capital allowance claim for private use. Instead the person who uses the car (e.g. the director) pays income tax on the benefit in kind.

The benefit in kind charge will be somewhere between 0% (zero CO_2 emissions) and 35% of the original purchase cost of the car when new. Furthermore, the company will have to pay employer's national insurance at 13.8% on the benefit in kind.

The tax on company cars has been steadily increasing in recent years and is only set to get worse. Any business owner who relies on their car for business should be sure to take account of the different tax rules that would apply if they use a company.

In extreme cases, the difference could be enough to make using a company less tax efficient overall.

Selling the Car

A key difference between self-employed businesses and companies is the capital allowance treatment when the car is sold.

Cars owned by sole traders and partnerships are treated as stand-alone assets for capital allowances purposes (provided there is some private use of the vehicle, which there usually is).

This means that, when the car is sold, a balancing allowance is available if the car is sold for less than its tax written down value. This is often the case because most cars lose value at a faster rate than 8% per year!

A balancing allowance essentially makes up for any shortfall in the car's capital allowances. The balancing allowance reduces your taxable profits and therefore reduces your tax bill.

Cars purchased by companies are not treated as separate stand-alone assets. Cars entitled to an 18% writing down allowance are added to the 'general pool' of assets. Cars entitled to an 8% writing down allowance are added to the 'special rate pool' of assets.

This means that, when the car is sold, there will NOT be a big balancing allowance to help reduce the company's tax bill. Instead, the outstanding balance remaining after deducting the car's sale proceeds will continue to attract capital allowances at 8% or 18%, along with other assets inside the pool.

Example

Gordon, a sole trader, buys a car and uses it 75% for business purposes and 25% privately. The car attracts capital allowances of 8% per year. Let's say the car's written down value is currently £25,000.

Gordon then sells the car for just £10,000. This gives rise to a balancing allowance of £11,250:

£25,000 - £10,000 = £15,000
£15,000 x 75% business use = £11,250

This means Gordon can claim a tax deduction of £11,250, saving him £4,725 in tax (at 42%) if he is a higher-rate taxpayer.

This example illustrates one of the key differences between sole traders/partnerships and companies.

Even though Gordon, a sole trader, is only allowed to claim a capital allowance of 8% per year, he can claim a big catch-up tax deduction when he sells the car. He would not be able to claim this balancing allowance if he was using a company. The company would have to continue claiming tax relief at just 8% per year.

Sole traders and partnerships are also not able to claim these big catch-up tax deductions for cars given to their employees or if their own cars have no private use.

Mileage Rates

Company Owners

Company owners who use their own cars for business journeys can receive tax-free business mileage payments from the company (the company can also claim the amount as a tax deduction). Business mileage can be claimed at the following rates:

- 45p per mile (first 10,000 miles)
- 25p per mile thereafter

Many company owners use the mileage rates instead of getting their company to buy a car for their use. This allows them to avoid company car benefit-in-kind tax charges, which are often extremely high. However, for those travelling well over 10,000 miles per year on business, the 25p per mile rate will not provide adequate compensation for the car's depreciation.

Example

Patrick, a company owner, travels 15,000 miles per year on business. He can claim the following tax-free mileage payment from his company:

- *10,000 x 45p = £4,500*
- *5,000 x 25p = £1,250*

Patrick's total tax-free payment for the year will be £5,750. The company can claim the amount as a tax deduction.

Self-Employed Business Owners

Self-employed business owners can also use the above mileage rates and the amount will be allowed as a tax deduction for the business (previously the mileage rates could only be used by businesses with turnover under the VAT threshold).

The mileage allowances can also be claimed for vans and other goods vehicles and motor cycles (the rate for motor cycles is 24p per mile).

Capital allowances cannot be claimed in addition to the mileage allowances. Furthermore, the mileage rates cannot be used if capital allowances have already been claimed for the vehicle.

The mileage allowances also cannot be used for goods vehicles and motor cycles if any of the cost of the vehicle has enjoyed tax relief under the cash basis (see Chapter 32).

As an alternative to the mileage allowances, self-employed business owners can claim capital allowances and their actual motoring costs (fuel, insurance, repairs etc), with a suitable reduction to reflect private use of the vehicle.

The mileage rates may have the advantage of simplicity but which method produces a bigger tax deduction? Sometimes your actual motoring expenses will produce the biggest tax deduction, sometimes the mileage rates – it all depends on your personal circumstances.

The amounts at stake are potentially significant and could amount to thousands of pounds per year. The two most important factors influencing your choice are arguably:

- The cost of your car
- The amount of business mileage

The more expensive your car is, the more important it is to claim capital allowances, which means you will also claim your actual motoring costs.

Chapter 34

Selling Your Business

One of the most tax-efficient ways to grow your wealth is to build and then sell several businesses during your working life.

This allows you to convert streams of heavily taxed income into low-taxed capital gains.

Many self-employed business owners and company owners face a marginal tax rate of at least 40% (including corporation tax if you're a company owner).

But, when you sell a business and receive a big cash lump sum, which replaces all this heavily taxed income, you could end up paying less than 10% tax if you qualify for Entrepreneurs' Relief.

Entrepreneurs' Relief can save a couple up to £3.6 million in capital gains tax, so it's worth knowing what you have to do to protect it.

How Entrepreneurs' Relief Works

Up to £10 million of capital gains per person can qualify for Entrepreneurs' Relief.

This is a lifetime limit but can be used for more than one business sale.

Sole traders, partnerships and company owners may all potentially qualify but, in each case, the business has to be what the taxman refers to as a 'trade'. Generally speaking this means that investment businesses (e.g. property investment businesses) do not qualify.

Sole traders are generally only entitled to Entrepreneurs' Relief when they sell the whole business (or shut it down and sell off the assets). If you continue trading but sell some business assets, for example a piece of intellectual property or your trading premises, you will not be entitled to any Entrepreneurs' Relief.

Company owners can benefit from Entrepreneurs' Relief when they sell shares in the company. There is no Entrepreneurs' Relief, however, if the company itself sells the underlying business or other assets. Instead the company will pay corporation tax and there may be additional tax payable by the company owner if any of the funds are extracted.

So if you own a company, from a tax-planning perspective, it's normally preferable to sell the company (ie your shares) rather than have the company sell the underlying business or assets owned (although a buyer may shy away from buying the company itself for fear of taking on any unexpected liabilities).

To qualify for Entrepreneurs' Relief the business must have been owned for at least one year. This is a critical point to remember if you are currently self employed and thinking of converting your business into a company.

Tax Planning Pointers

Beware of Incorporating

If you have a sole trader business or partnership, you should be wary of incorporating (putting the business into a company) within one year of selling. To qualify for Entrepreneurs' Relief, you have to own the shares of the newly formed company for at least one year.

Be Wary of Business Transfers to Family Members

Transfers to spouses are exempt from CGT and can save significant amounts of income tax. However, if the business is sold less than one year after the transfer, Entrepreneurs' Relief will not be available on the transferred share unless the spouse already held a share of the business before that (and for at least a year prior to the sale).

Chapter 35

Business Property

Self Employed

Many sole traders own their own premises (offices, shops, warehouses etc). They can't pay themselves rent but many of their property expenses (e.g. mortgage interest, repairs, insurance etc) are all allowed as a tax deduction against the profits of the business, allowing the sole trader to pay less income tax and national insurance.

Business partners can rent property to the partnership. Charging the partnership rent will reduce the taxable profits of the business and allow the partners to receive rental income which avoids national insurance.

If the property is sold for a profit, capital gains tax may be payable at either 18% (basic-rate taxpayers) or 28% (higher-rate taxpayers).

However, business owners often qualify for two special capital gains tax reliefs:

- Rollover Relief
- Entrepreneurs' Relief

Rollover Relief can be claimed if you move to different trading premises. Effectively it lets you postpone paying capital gains tax on the old property until the new property is sold. This gives the business flexibility to grow without adverse tax consequences.

You can buy the new property between a year before and three years after selling the original property. All of the old property's sale proceeds must be reinvested. Any shortfall is deducted from the amount of gain eligible for rollover. Relief is also restricted if there is less than full trading use of the property.

Entrepreneurs' Relief allows you to pay capital gains tax at just 10%. However, it can generally only be claimed as part of an overall sale of the business. You cannot claim it for a stand-alone sale of business premises.

Company Owners

Business properties can be owned by either:

- The company
- The company owner

If the property belongs to the company owner, the company can pay him rent. Provided the rent is not excessive, the company will enjoy corporation tax relief on these rent payments.

However, rent is not mandatory: there is no requirement for a company owner to charge it. Paying rent is, however, often tax efficient if the company owner has tax-deductible expenses (e.g. mortgage interest) that can be offset against the rental income.

Charging rent will, however, reduce the amount of Entrepreneurs' Relief you can claim (see below).

Selling the Property

Rollover Relief is available both for properties owned by companies and company owners themselves.

The same goes for Entrepreneurs' Relief – it can be claimed for properties owned by companies and company owners themselves. This lets you pay capital gains tax at just 10%. However, there has to be an overall sale of the business to qualify.

Furthermore, if you own the property personally and your company pays you rent, you will not be entitled to the maximum amount of Entrepreneurs' Relief. (The same goes for properties rented to partnerships.) The taxman's reasoning is that, if the property is only available to the business if rent is paid, it is an investment asset and not a business asset.

There are two pieces of good news here though. Firstly, any rent receivable before April 2008 is disregarded and, secondly, rent paid at less than the market rate only leads to a partial reduction in the available Entrepreneurs' Relief.

For example, the gain on a property owned since 5 April 2005 and rented to the owner's company for 50% of market rent until its sale (as part of a larger business sale) nine years later, on 5 April 2014, would have its Entrepreneurs' Relief restricted by a factor of 6/9 x 50% = 33.33%. For example, if the gain were £100,000, relief could be claimed on £66,667 of that gain.

What happens if the company owns the property? If the buyer of the business wants the property included in the sale, you could sell your shares in the company and all of the proceeds may qualify for Entrepreneurs' Relief.

However, an expensive property asset may put off prospective buyers who don't need it (e.g. if the business being sold is not reliant on a specific property – think internet company rather than restaurant). The property may then have to be sold first with corporation tax payable on the capital gain and income tax paid when the money is extracted from the company prior to the sale.

Stand-alone Sales

What if there is a stand-alone sale of the property and no Rollover Relief claim (because the proceeds are not used to buy another property) and no Entrepreneurs' Relief claim (because the business is not being sold)?

A few years ago, companies potentially paid a lot more tax on property capital gains than individuals. This is not necessarily the case any longer.

Individuals who are higher-rate taxpayers pay up to 28% capital gains tax. Companies currently pay corporation tax at 20% on up to £300,000 of profits. From April 2015 all companies will pay 20% corporation tax on all of their profits, including property sales.

So if you are a higher-rate taxpayer, your company will generally pay less tax than you would (20% versus 28%).

The first £11,000 of an individual's capital gains are tax free thanks to the annual exemption. Companies instead enjoy indexation relief which is potentially much more valuable. For a property costing £300,000, indexation relief could shelter around £100,000 of the gain from tax if the property is sold in 10 years' time.

Inheritance Tax

Shares in private trading companies or the value of a partnership interest in a trade or profession are generally exempt from inheritance tax.

A property held personally but used by such a company or partnership, only attracts 50% relief, leaving inheritance tax payable at an effective rate of 20% on the property's value. Any mortgage against the property reduces the tax, however, as you only pay inheritance tax on your net wealth.

Generally, you can transfer the property to the company or partnership before you die and then get the full relief but there's always the risk that you won't get the chance to do this and most transfers come at some sort of tax cost.

Non-tax Factors

- **Insolvency**. As a company owner, one of the benefits of holding your business premises personally is that, if the company becomes insolvent, a property owned by the director personally should be safe from creditors (unless fraud or negligence is involved).

- **Mortgages**. You may find it more difficult to find an attractive mortgage deal if the property is owned by your company.

- **Retirement**. Many company owners view the business premises as their pension – available to rent to their old company or another business after they retire.

Chapter 36

Borrowing Money

New companies sometimes struggle to raise finance. However, it's important to point out that, as a company owner, you can borrow money *personally* and invest it or lend it to your company and personally claim tax relief on the interest.

You can claim tax relief for the interest you pay as a deduction against *any* taxable income you have, eg salary income, dividends and interest.

For example, a company owner could borrow against their home, lend the money to their company and all of the interest can be claimed against the company owner's taxable income from all sources.

This tax deduction is known as 'qualifying loan interest'.

Qualifying loan interest may allow you to enjoy tax relief at 40% if you are a higher-rate taxpayer. Most small companies only enjoy corporation tax relief at 20% on their interest charges.

Example

Guy, a higher-rate taxpayer, borrows money personally and lends it to his company. Guy's interest bill on the borrowed funds comes to £10,000. Guy also has investment income of £20,000 from other sources. His interest bill can be set off against his investment income, resulting in an income tax saving of £4,000 (£10,000 x 40%).

If the company itself borrowed the money, it would only enjoy corporation tax relief of £2,000 (£10,000 x 20%).

Qualifying Loan Interest – Who Can Use It?

There are some restrictions on who can benefit from this tax relief:

- The company must be a close company, i.e. under the control of five people or less. Most private companies are close companies.

- The investor must generally own 5% or more of the company's share capital. Shares owned by close family members are usually counted but you must own at least some shares yourself.

- The company must carry on a qualifying activity, including a trade or profession or property letting business.

There are also restrictions on the amount of tax relief available. From 6 April 2013 onwards there is an annual limit on the total amount of income tax relief available from various tax reliefs, including this one (see Chapter 31).

The total amount of relief is being limited to the *greater* of:

- £50,000, or
- 25% of your 'adjusted total income'

Drawbacks

One of the dangers of borrowing money personally is that personal debts are not protected by the company's limited liability status. In practice, however, most banks insist on personal guarantees from small company directors anyway, so either way you will probably be personally exposed if you borrow money for your company.

Another problem with borrowing money personally is that you may not have enough personal income from other sources to service the debt.

For example, if the money you borrow is *invested* in your company (ie used to buy shares in your company), you may have to declare a dividend to service the personal debt. If income tax is payable on the dividend, this will eliminate the tax benefit of obtaining personal interest relief.

(Increasing your company's share capital may have other tax consequences too. For example it could increase the stamp duty payable if the company is sold. It may also be more difficult to get your money back, requiring some sort of company restructuring or share buy back. Tax charges and professional fees could make such exercises expensive.)

Lending Money to Your Company

Instead of investing the money in your company you can lend it to your company. Your company can pay you interest if this is required to service your personal debt.

This income will be taxable.

The company will be able to claim corporation tax relief on the interest, provided a commercial rate of interest is charged. If you do this, the company is required to deduct basic-rate tax and account for it to HMRC. The company owner can, however, reclaim it at a later date when they complete their own tax return.

It is often worth charging the maximum market rate applying because interest income can be more tax efficient than salaries or dividends.

One benefit of lending money to your company, as opposed to investing it, is that the money can be withdrawn at a later date with no adverse tax consequences.

Part 8

Setting Up Your Company

Chapter 37

How to Set Up a Company

The act of forming a company is known as 'incorporation'.

Setting up a company is extremely easy. There are several websites that let you complete the whole process online for just a couple of hundred pounds.

Many accountants and solicitors will also help you for a modest fee, although some charge in excess of £1,000.

Two documents are required to form a company:

- The memorandum of association
- The articles of association

The memorandum is a statement made by each subscriber confirming their intention to form a company and become a member of that company. If the company is to have a share capital on formation, each member also agrees to take at least one share.

The articles of association are the rules governing the running of the company, for example the rights of shareholders, the appointment and removal of directors, borrowing powers etc.

Ready-made 'model' articles of association apply when most companies are formed. However, it is possible to create your own personalised document, although this will involve extra fees.

All companies require a registered office address (PO boxes are not allowed). The company's name must be displayed at the registered address and its statutory books and records are usually kept there.

A UK company can be registered in Scotland, in Northern Ireland or in England and Wales, depending on where its registered office is located.

Appointing Directors

When you set up your company you will need to appoint at least one director. You may also need to appoint a company secretary. Directors and company secretaries are referred to as the company's 'officers'.

Companies House requires a home address for each officer. However, you can also provide a service address (for example, the company's registered address) which is the one that will appear in the public domain. This allows you to keep your home address private.

The company's shareholders are referred to as 'members'. A company must have at least one member.

Company Tax Compliance

After setting up your company you will receive a letter from HMRC advising you to register online on their website. This gets your company into the corporation tax system.

You will probably also need to register the company as an employer for PAYE purposes and possibly for VAT.

The company will automatically be provided with an 'accounting date'. This is essentially its tax year end. It will automatically be set to 12 months after the month end when the company was incorporated.

Your company's accounting date can generally be changed by submitting a form AA01 to Companies House. Speak to your accountant before doing this, however, because there are corporation tax consequences.

Banking

To start trading you will need to set up a bank account. Some banks will appoint you a dedicated business adviser who can complete this task for you quickly and with minimum fuss.

Most company accounts come with a cheque book and online banking but do not come with debit cards, which can make day to day transactions difficult.

The fees and charges are often higher than for personal accounts.

Company credit cards are available but the terms can be unattractive and many company owners use a dedicated personal card for company purchases.

Annual Returns & Accounts

Once your company is up and running you will have to submit two documents to Companies House each year:

- Annual accounts
- Annual return

The annual return contains details of the directors and shareholders. There are late-filing penalties but it is not a difficult task to complete online and the cost is minimal (£13).

Small companies do not have to submit a full set of statutory accounts to Companies House. Instead they can submit abbreviated accounts which contain a lot less detail, thereby maintaining their privacy (the abbreviated accounts are available to the public).

These accounts must generally be submitted within nine months of the end of the accounting period.

The full set of statutory accounts and a corporation tax return must be submitted to HMRC.

Chapter 38

Incorporating an Existing Business

Although it is relatively cheap and easy to set up a company, incorporating an *existing* sole trader business is more complicated and costly. The additional costs – professional adviser fees and tax charges – have to be weighed against the ongoing tax savings you hope to achieve from using a company.

It is essential to obtain professional advice before incorporating an existing business. This chapter contains a brief overview of some of the issues.

Capital Gains Tax

Capital gains tax is an important issue for businesses seeking to incorporate. Any transfer of assets between you and your company is deemed to take place at market value. This means you could face a large capital gains tax bill when you incorporate.

There are, however, two important capital gains tax reliefs that can solve this problem:

- Incorporation Relief
- Gift Relief

Incorporation Relief

To qualify for this relief:

- All of the assets of the business (excluding cash if desired) must be transferred to the company, and

- The business must be transferred as a going concern, and

- The business must be transferred wholly or partly in exchange for shares issued by the company to the person transferring the business.

The capital gain arising from the transfer of the assets is deducted from the individual's base cost in the company shares. This means that the transferor's base cost for the shares is the same as the base cost he previously had for the underlying assets.

Incorporation Relief is given automatically.

Gift Relief

Gift relief can be claimed as an alternative to Incorporation Relief. The advantage of this relief is that you do not have to transfer all of the assets into the company. Some assets can be kept outside the company.

The relief works by allowing the capital gain on the transfer to be 'held over'. This means that the individual making the transfer has no capital gains tax to pay but it also means that the assets transferred to the company have a lower base cost. The assets' base cost is reduced by the amount of gain held over.

Note that this relief is not automatic and a claim must be made jointly by the transferring taxpayer and the recipient company.

Example
Manos runs his e-commerce business from an office in Manchester. He decides to transfer the business, including the office which he owns personally, into a new company called Manos Manchester Ltd.

He bought the office for £200,000. Its current market value is £500,000. Manos decides to gift the property to Manos Manchester Ltd.

Normally Manos would have a capital gain of £300,000. However, if Manos and his company jointly elect to hold over the gain, Manos will not have to pay any capital gains tax. Manos Manchester Ltd will hold the property with a base cost of £200,000:

Market value	*£500,000*
Less: Gain held over	*£300,000*
Base cost	*£200,000*

The company ends up with the same base cost as the individual. If the company sells the property eventually it will pay corporation tax on the capital gain (calculated using a £200,000 base cost).

Rather than gifting assets like trading premises for no consideration, it may be worth selling them to the company. This may result in capital gains tax being payable but in many cases the individual will be entitled to Entrepreneurs' Relief (10% capital gains tax).

The company can pay for the property by crediting the director's loan account. This amount can then be withdrawn tax free later on (ie with no income tax or national insurance).

For higher-rate taxpayers, paying 10% capital gains tax is far more attractive than the tax payable on salaries and dividends.

Other business owners prefer to retain *personal* ownership of their trading premises. This allows them to receive rental income payments from the company and protects the property from commercial risks (ie creditors) and protects them from paying stamp duty land tax.

Personal ownership of trading premises has its drawbacks, however. For example, if the company is sold, where rent has been paid by the company to the company owner, the amount of Entrepreneurs' Relief available for the property will be restricted (possibly no relief will be allowed if a full market rent has been paid). For inheritance tax purposes only 50% business property relief is allowed for properties owned personally.

Goodwill

Care needs to be taken when valuing the goodwill that is to be transferred to the new company. A reasonable valuation will have to be agreed with HMRC's Shares and Assets Office.

Again, a popular tax-planning strategy is to sell the goodwill to the company (rather than use the two tax reliefs described above). Even if this means taking a small capital gains tax hit now, the amount can be credited to the director's loan account and withdrawn tax free later on.

Stamp Duty Land Tax

If you are a sole trader and decide to transfer your trading premises to your company, the transfer will be subject to stamp duty land tax. This tax is payable even if the property is transferred for no consideration because the company and the sole trader are treated as connected persons. In other words, the company is deemed to have paid the market value for the property for stamp duty purposes.

Although there is no stamp duty on goodwill, some property-based businesses may see the value of their transferred properties increased for stamp duty land tax purposes to reflect the inherent goodwill attaching to the property (i.e. the goodwill that arises from the location of the property).

Even if you do not transfer business premises to your company, stamp duty land tax may still be payable if you decide to lease the property to the company. However, in many cases SDLT can be avoided by granting the company a non-exclusive licence to occupy the property.

Lightning Source UK Ltd.
Milton Keynes UK
UKOW06f0343130216

268297UK00001B/66/P